DEM●S

Demos is an independent think-tank committed to radical thinking on the long-term problems facing the UK and other advanced industrial societies.

It aims to develop ideas – both theoretical and practical – to help shape the politics of the 21st century, and to improve the breadth and quality of political debate.

Demos publishes books and a quarterly journal and undertakes substantial empirical and policy-oriented research projects. Demos is a registered charity.

In all its work Demos brings together people from a wide range of backgrounds in business, academia, government, the voluntary sector and the media to share and cross-fertilise ideas and experiences.

For further information and subscription details please write to:
Demos
9 Bridewell Place
London, EC4V 6AP
Telephone: 0171 353 4479
Facsimile: 0171 353 4481
email: joanna@demos.demon.co.uk

On the Cards

Privacy, identity and trust in the age of smart technologies

Perri 6 and Ivan Briscoe

First published in 1996 by
Demos
9 Bridewell Place
London EC4V 6AP
Telephone: 0171 353 4479
Facsimile: 0171 353 4481
e-mail: joanna@demos.demon.co.uk
© Demos 1996

All rights reserved
Paper No. 20
ISBN 1 898309 72 8
Printed in Great Britain by
EG Bond Ltd
Designed by Esterson Lackersteen
Typeset by Wade Associates
Thanks to Adrian Taylor

Contents

Summary 9

Introduction 15

Smartening up 19

What is a smart card?

Benefits for individuals

Benefits for organisations

Who is playing card games? 28

Take-up and take-off

Financial services: 'electronic cash'

Health care

Transport

Retail sector: 'loyalty cards'

Telecommunications

Government and the public sector

Smart futures: drivers of change 39

Technology

Business demand

Government demand

Regulation of cryptography

Consumers

Single application cards

Issuer consortium-controlled multi-functional cards

Consumer-controlled multi functional cards

Trust and the politics of privacy 52

The information society, risk and privacy

Public fears

Reassurance from business and technology interests

The civil libertarian case

Balancing risk and reason

A case of mistaken identity? A government card 73

The consultation paper

The debate

Trust and surveillance

Privacy, power and law 79

Principles of privacy

Data protection law

Evaluation data protection law today

Smart privacy: policy solutions 87

Regulating strong cryptography

Privacy-enhancing technologies (PETs)

Principles of a data protection régime for the smart technology age

Regulating the market structure for trust: structural separation

Learning from experience about how to implement separation

Citizen ownership: personal data and cards

Conclusion 108

Glossary 111

Notes 120

Acknowledgements

We are especially grateful to Francis Aldhouse, Mark Gordon, Anne Hinde, Richard Poynder and Charles Raab, who commented on an earlier draft of the text. As part of the research conducted for the writing of this book, the authors interviewed, either in person or over the telephone, a wide range of experts in various aspects of the issues we discuss. We are deeply grateful to them for the time they made available, and for the information they gave us. We hope they will recognise in the book the contribution they have made to our thinking. None of our views – and certainly none of our errors – should be attributed to any of these people. Those whom we interviewed are, in alphabetical order:

Francis Aldhouse, Office of the Data Protection Registrar; Ram Banerjee, independent consultant; David Birch, Hyperion; Robert Cablehorn, Mondex; Simon Davies, Privacy International; David Everett, independent consultant, consultant to NatWest, editor of Smart Card News; Conor Foley, then of Liberty; Colin Fricker, Direct Marketing Association; Mark Gordon, Mondex; William Heath, Kable; Anne Hinde, Office of the Data Protection Registrar; Vanessa Houlder, *Financial Times;* Melanie Howard, Henley Centre for Forecasting; Richard Johnston, Associated Payment and Clearing Systems; Barry Kelly, Office of the Data Protection Registrar; Frank Lovell, Central Computer and Telecommunications Agency; Nick Platten, Directorate-General XV of the European Commission; Richard Poynder, Smart Card Club; Charles Raab, Department of Politics, University of Edinburgh; Martin Robson, Central Computer and Telecommunications Agency; John Stevens, MEP; Karen Swinden, Kable; Gary Waller MP; and John Worsfold, consultant.

Summary

Over the next few years the number and importance of **smart cards** is set to rise dramatically. Some will be provided by private companies, such as banks and retailers; some by governments using them either as identity cards or to assist in health and social security; others may be provided by non-profit organisations.

Such cards offer numerous potential **benefits**, both for individuals and for organisations. But their introduction raises major challenges to existing data protection law and to our fundamental ideas about **privacy**. As the flows of data rise relentlessly in 'information society' of the next century, the questions of how personal control and 'smart privacy' can be created will dominate public policy debates. Smart cards will be the first, the most tangible and the most visible focus for these debates.

So far, however, the debate has been largely polarised between civil libertarians – who tend to oppose any greater use of smart technologies – and those in government and businesses who too often dismiss concerns about misuse of information out of hand.

This book argues that neither position is helpful, and that instead we need a new framework to govern smart cards, and information more generally, to ensure the

Summary

maximum public benefit from a set of new technologies, and credible guarantees that information will not be misused. It sets out a strategy for securing reasonable privacy that relies on market-based instruments and the lightest possible regulation. The argument goes as follows.

First, we analyse the factors likely to shape the *smart card revolution*. We argue that the future of smart cards will be determined by technological developments, the changing and growing patterns of business and government, trends in regulation of the encryption systems used in the cards, and the extent to which consumers trust smart card systems, not least in respecting confidentiality of personal data. In a few years, we can expect on the market single application cards, multi-functional cards issued by consortia of companies and government departments and perhaps multi-functional cards owned by consumers, where consumers decide for themselves which applications they will put on which cards, much as we do today with floppy disks.

Second, we examine questions of **public trust**. Research from the UK and North America suggests that consumers and citizens are at the very least cautious and in some cases suspicious of the implications of the smart card economy for privacy. They fear, first, the accumulation of personal information that lies behind the cards. Secondly, they fear that multi-functional cards could grant some agencies that hold and process personal information – 'data users' – access to personal information not intended for them. At least some government agencies are trusted significantly less than many businesses. A clear hierarchy of personal information emerges that people are decreasingly unwilling to hand over, even in return for services.

Third, we analyse the currently dominant **policy arguments**. Business, government and technology voices offer reassurance that password, biometric checking, and encryption technologies will ensure more privacy than ever before. Business people often argue that they have no commercial reason for behaving like Big Brother and that consumers will choose to do business only with companies that respect privacy. They go on to say that the public generally report concerns only about the consequences of loss of cards, not about privacy. Civil libertarians reply that there are reasons to expect a wide and intrusive variety of types of personal information to be stored and accessed from smart cards, and used – sometimes by incorrect inferences – to determine how people are to be treated. They point to commercial reasons why business has an interest in extensive surveillance, in the value of consumer profile information and the market for it, and to traditional governmental tendencies toward authoritarianism. They argue that technology alone will not guarantee security, not least because decryption keys may be traded between companies and government agencies without the knowledge of the consumer or citizen. The only reason that people do not report privacy concerns in market research, they argue, is that they are poorly informed about the risks: when better informed, they become concerned. The market will not automatically select privacy-respecting companies, because consumers do not have sufficient information to choose them, and the mechanism certainly does not work with government. They document a wide range of abuses, and point to the violations of privacy and the risks of error and mistreatment arising from data matching and data mining, and enforced disclosure of personal information. Smart cards are not an unique source of these evils but they present a new and more frequent source of old risks, and once they are accepted, they will acquire new roles by 'function creep'.

Fourth, we argue that both positions are implausibly extreme. Some civil libertarians may not understand the nature of the new cryptographic techniques, and some seem to conflate arguments about the desirable extent of risk pooling between individuals with arguments about privacy. Nevertheless, there are real risks of abuse. These will be sharpest in the case of multi-functional smart cards.

Fifth, we show how these debates play out in the case of proposals for **government identity cards**. The British government has yet to announce whether it will introduce an identity card, and if so, whether it will be a smart card, and whether it would be a multi-functional card for a wide variety of public sector applications, and whether it would be open to business to rent space in the chip for their own applications. The Conservative election manifesto may contain some commitment. Such a multi-functional card would quickly become *de facto* compulsory, even if neither police nor courts could draw conclusions from anyone's refusal to produce one. It would also be a major force for centralisation in government, and could represent a quantum step in the levels of surveillance.

Sixth, we set out our **framework of policy goals**. We argue that the aim of public policy should be to buttress two crucial privacy rights:

● the right to remain anonymous, at least in certain transactions where it is not necessary for the purpose of the transaction to be fulfilled, that the other party knows who one is;

● the right to control the uses others make of personal information they hold about one, that is, to consent to certain uses and to veto certain others.

The present policy régime in Britain does not suffice to secure these rights.

The heart of the **present policy paradigm** is data protection law, in the form of the 1984 Data Protection Act and legislation to be brought forward shortly to implement the 1995 European Directive. However, the present set of data protection laws are not adequate to control modern data matching and data mining techniques; in some cases are drafted so widely as to be almost unenforceable; provide limited rights for individuals to require deletion and correction; leave action in the hands of the data user or the regulator and not the individual data subject; in most cases provide rights after the event; set up a largely passive system of regulation; provide no support for the use of privacy-enhancing technologies; and have wide exemptions.

We propose to broaden the policy framework for achieving these two key rights, by strengthening data protection law; creating a structurally separate and independent market in data access services as a discipline on data users; creating an ownership régime under which individuals can choose to make up their own multi-functional smart cards by buying blank cards with privacy-respecting architectures from agencies that they trust; promoting the use of privacy-enhancing technologies; and re-thinking the approach to regulation of strong cryptography.

First, **data protection law** should be based on the principle that unless the data subject expressly consents to a specific use or disclosure of personal information, that use or disclosure should not be permitted, except in the core functions of government concerned with security and law enforcement. Data subjects should have the right of independent access to their records. We also propose a range of measures to tighten up the present duties and exemptions and to control data matching.

Second, **a structural separation law** should be introduced that would create a separate category of data access services. Data user agencies would not be permitted more than small ownership stakes in data access companies, and they would have to allow data access companies the means to provide individuals with accurate and comprehensive views of what is held about them, and, where appropriate, to make corrections and deletions. Even if there is not sufficient demand to sustain many or even any data access companies in the market, the law would provide a discipline analogous to the way that 'contestability' does for monopolists. We set out key principles for implementing structural separation, which are drawn from the experience of cross-media ownership, competition and financial services regulation.

Summary

Third, in case the market does not spontaneously offer consumers **multi-functional cards** over which they have ownership rights, allowing only those applications to co-reside where they trust the issuing companies and government departments not to abuse the opportunity to 'peek' at each other's data, then government should require that consumer-owned multi-functional cards be made available alongside issuer-owned cards.

Fourth, if data users (such as hospitals or credit rating agencies) do not use **privacy-enhancing technologies** which make it possible to guarantee anonymity except where it is absolutely necessary to use someone's real identity, government should take powers to persuade, offer incentives and if necessary to compel them to do so.

Fifth, whatever the national security arguments, in our view, there is no point in trying to prohibit private individuals and companies from having access to **strong cryptography**. However, we argue that there should be regulation to encourage a voluntary system of independent, non-governmental registries that would hold, on a confidential basis, companies' and individuals' cryptographic keys; government law enforcement agencies would need a court order to gain access to these keys.

This distinctive five-pronged strategy represents a clear and sensible course, and it avoids errors of the extreme civil libertarian position and the unconvincing bland assurances of some business and technology advocates. We propose light touch market-based instruments of regulation; a clear alternative to the authoritarian vision of a government-issued and owned card as the base of the market; assurance for civil liberties; and a strong platform for business to offer services to consumers that will enhance their lives while also enhancing their privacy.

Introduction

Politicians and the media everywhere are debating what the 'information society' could mean.[1] Smart cards, enabling us all to access everything 'on-line' over the 'information superhighway', are being spoken about in tones that range from the visionary to the technocratic.

As more and more information flows around the cables that make the modern economy truly global, as more information is copied between disk and CD-ROMs, and as new ways to connect with the databases and highways proliferate – from traditional computers through to palm-top devices and card-sized computers – the issues of the confidentiality and privacy of personal information will become ever more important in political life.

The issues with which this book deals are not just important for technology buffs or banks. They are issues that will appear in party election manifestos for many years to come, and around which both social movements and new industries will be organised. They go both to the heart of the co-ordination of our governmental system, and to the nature of ordinary people's relationships with the big institutions that shape our lives.

Unfortunately, most public debate, even in the more sophisticated broadsheet press, consists in eulogies to the dream world to come, or else grand jeremiads against the Orwellian nightmare around the corner. Neither kind of discussion is much use.

Part of the problem is that our information politics remain firmly in the twentieth century even as our technology and our problems are becoming those of a new age. The conflict between libertarians and authoritarians will never be settled once and for all. However, neither side offers positions that have caught up with technical change. Both sides are still concerned mainly with the state. Libertarians want to guard privacy against the action of governmental agencies, and authoritarians want to ensure that such privacy claims do not undermine what they see as the duty of the individual to be ruled,[2] or that privacy does not provide cover for crime, terrrorism and subversion. Neither side has yet understood the implications for their politics of the role of business and the new markets in information. The result is a political confrontation resembling a Punch and Judy show.

This can be seen in the current debate about government-issued identity cards. In 1995, the Home Secretary, the Rt. Hon. Michael Howard MP, published a consultation paper on the options for identity cards that might be issued by government: one choice may be a smart card. At the time of writing, it is still not clear what, if anything, the government will settle upon, but it seems likely that something will appear in the Conservative Party manifesto.

The arguments for such a card were straightforwardly authoritarian. It was claimed that it would reduce crime, illegal immigration, benefit fraud, and various other evils. Few of those claims have withstood scrutiny. The opponents were conventional civil libertarians who at times seemed to take a simple Luddite stand against any information technology for fear that it would erode privacy.

However, neither side in the political debate has paid much attention to the fact that many of us carry more and more identity cards with us. Most are privately issued and in at least some cases, many people welcomed them, as consumers. These smart cards are but one part of the wider information and communication technologies that are transforming our world. Yet they are important, not least because the smart card is set to become the consumer or citizen's portable key to the information economy, as well as the key to many basic services already on offer. Smart technologies raise privacy issues that are hardly touched by traditional state-centred debates about privacy or by other privacy debates such as those about the intrusiveness of the press, or about the merits or otherwise of closed circuit television in public places. Even business has yet to appreciate the potential scale of the privacy issues that these technologies raise.

It is time, therefore, to examine seriously the implications of smart card technology as a way to understand what privacy might mean in the coming information society.

In this book, we set out the case for a new approach to the issues of privacy and personal data control for the information society and we offer an approach to making privacy and the new information market work together in harmony. We examine first the nature of the information technology, and the benefits that it offers. Next, we review the main applications to which it has been put by business and government, and we go on to look at the main 'drivers of change' that will shape the future use of the technology.

In the second half of the book, we turn to the fears the public has, and look at how the two sides of the conventional debate respond to them, offering our own assessment of the strengths and weaknesses of each side's case. Then, we set out our five-pronged strategy for creating harmony between privacy and information markets. We suggest detailed reforms to the regulation of cryptography and to data protection law, a range of policies to stimulate the use of privacy-enhancing technologies, a radical new market-based proposal for disciplining agencies that do not convince the public of their trustworthiness, and a proposal to put more control and ownership rights over cards in the hands of consumers.

Smartening up

What is a smart card?

Basically, a smart card is a tiny computer. Although in this book, we talk mainly about cards, in principle, the tiny computer could be embedded in anything portable – a watch, a hatpin, an earring, a pen. It is merely for convenience, and because most of us are used to carrying other kinds of cards around, that most companies use a wallet-sized plastic card. Cards are the individual's keys to the new information and communications systems, and the most tangible expression of the new age.

A smart card, then, is a portable, credit card-sized device that carries a tiny chip with the capacity not just to store information, but to process it according to instructions. That capacity is activated when the card is in contact with another device, usually to carry out a transaction. For example, smart cards can check the right of any device seeking access to the data on the chip, change data in response to certain instructions during a transaction, and manage security procedures such as the operations of passwords or encryption software, to prevent unauthorised users from gaining access. In practice, this means that the chip can authenticate the card to a reader device, check the validity of the reader device, and carry information about the cardholder for use in transactions or services.

Memory and processor cards

The simplest case is the 'memory-only' card. In this case, the chip is used only for the storage of larger quantities of electronically coded information than could conveniently be stored in some other portable form, such as the magnetic stripe on the obverse of a typical credit card. Any operations performed on that information are carried out by the devices that read the information in the card.

More complex are 'micro-processor' cards, where the chip in the card conducts some of the work of reading, writing, calculating, etc with the information stored in the card or elsewhere. These cards can respond to external events, making their own 'decisions' about where to store data, whether to allow data to be read, or when they will allow information to be transferred in and out.[3]

On-line and off-line

A card can be used in two ways to carry out a transaction. All the information necessary for the transaction may be stored in the card and read from it (and perhaps re-written during the transaction) by a reader device. In this case, it is not necessary for the reader device to contact – usually over the telephone wire system – a remote central database. This is therefore known as an 'off-line' transaction. Alternatively, the card may contain very little personal information, beyond that which is necessary to check that that particular card is authorised to engage in the transaction. Rather, it will contain a set of instructions for granting access to remote centrally held records, during a call made across the network.

Contact and contactless

The chip in the card can deal with the reader device in one of two ways. 'Contact cards' are ones that are physically inserted into the device and the circuit between the two physically connected. 'Contactless cards' are passed in front of the device at a distance, and power is sent from the reader device over a distance of several metres to activate the chip in the card.

Smart cards vary widely in their powers of processing and memory: the forms in which they are used depend more than anything on the context of their use, and the benefits sought for individuals and the organisations that issue the cards.

Benefits for individuals
Smart card technology offers real gains in convenience, time and, in some cases, safety. For individuals, smart cards could provide a range of benefits.

A secure means of authenticating one's own identity
For many transactions with business and government, one must prove one's identity, in order to demonstrate one's eligibility for a particular service. Both public and private service providers are rightly concerned to minimise the risk of loss from impersonation. The use of a Personal Identification Number (PIN) is often not sufficient to prove the identity of the cardholder because PINs can be obtained by unauthorised users. Something more may be required.

Cards can store not only the name, address and PIN of the individual to whom they are granted, but also biometric information that enables a check to be made by the reader device against the individual presenting the card. Biometrics include a basic photograph of the face, a stored image of a fingerprint (as is the case with the new Spanish social security card), digitised hand geometry, the voice pattern, the retina or, if higher levels of security are required but instant checking is not, DNA information.

At present, however, such cards are not common. This is because the technology needed for an off-line reader device to read a complex biometric such as a fingerprint, and then to read the cardholder's fingerprint and compare the two is complex, expensive and not yet as fast as retailers would like. Visual checks by individual retailers of photographs, signatures or fingerprints are prone to error.

A signature can be used as a biometric, with a reader device comparing the way that the signature is produced during the transaction with one stored in digital form (this is known as the 'dynamic signature'). However, at the moment, these systems issue an unacceptably large number of incorrect rejections. Some commentators speculate that voice recognition software will develop to the point that reader devices will become voice-based, and enable individuals to interact directly with central databases in a secure setting, without even the medium of the smart card.

A secure means of authenticating the identity of a reader device and system
Cardholders need to be assured that when they present their cards for some transaction, the reader device is valid, and belongs to the company they want to deal with. This is the basic level of consumer protection against fraud. Most smart cards use a security system that requires the reader device to present a valid code before the card allows the transaction to proceed or data on the card (or on a remote central database to which the card acts as the gatekeeper) to be accessed.

Speedier transactions
The electronic processes involved in chip-to-chip exchange are, at least in principle, much faster than those involved in physical handing over of notes and coins or handing over and reading of paper documentation, or even in reading a magnetic stripe. Therefore, cards could bring significant time savings, reduced queuing and much speedier follow-through on transactions, such as the provision of quotations or the delivery of additional forms. In some cases, the speed of transactions could be a matter of life or death. For example, if road accident

victims carried smart cards granting authorised medical personnel access to certain parts of their medical records, such as blood group, contagious disease status, etc, then appropriate and prompt treatment could be provided in many more cases. Naturally, this would require that ambulance staff would have to carry reader devices, and there would have to be some reliable means, perhaps using a biometric check, of verifying quickly that the card is that of the accident victim and is up to date. However, these are, in principle, soluble problems.

A portable and secure store of information
The miniaturisation of chips used in smart cards allows people to carry around much larger quantities of information than is otherwise practical. At present, many people carry forms of identity information that grant them access to certain buildings, forms of financial information that grant them access to their bank or building society accounts or their share trading accounts, information about their willingness to have bodily organs used after their death in case of accident, and even larger volumes of more frequently updated information in their diaries, address books and floppy disks. In principle, much of this could be miniaturised and placed on directories on a smart card. This may not, at least initially, be of much use for frequently updated information, but as the price of personal reading and writing machines falls and as the storage capacity of chips on cards rises, this may prove worthwhile.

Secure access to on-line services
The advent of the Internet and other networks means that many more purchases and other transactions will be conducted remotely using calls, typically using the telephone network. Technologies have already been devised by IBM and other companies using smart cards to control access to computer resources, through comparison of a signature with the signature stored in the card.[4] As on-line services develop, smart cards will

provide the main technological resource for secure identification and fraud protection, using encrypted access keys to authenticate a cardholder's right to access particular remotely held central databases. This might prove particularly useful with the advent of home shopping, where the use of secure media is essential. Smart encryption technology is also the obvious means to complement the use of security systems over the Internet. Although fraudsters are not likely to concentrate their efforts on intercepting individual credit card numbers of authentication codes as they are transmitted, they may "hack" into central databases of customer records containing credit card details held by big organisations, and use the Internet to make transactions using those credit card details, unless encryption systems both on the original cards and on central databases are sufficiently tight to prevent this.

Possibilities of more sophisticated off-line transactions
Smart cards can be used to carry out transactions without the initiation of an on-line connection to centrally held data. In countries such as Russia, where the telephone network is still of poor quality or limited coverage, it clearly makes sense to use cards for off-line transactions wherever possible. Even in countries such as the USA, where the telephone network is good, the volume of traffic over the twisted pair copper wiring system can reach a point where queuing begins to develop. In the absence of fibre-optic coverage for much of the population, off-line transactions may therefore be quicker and cheaper in many cases. Naturally, at some point, records held on distributed cards and records held centrally will have to be reconciled, but this need not necessarily be done during each transaction.

Simplicity
Smart cards can carry information permitting transactions of more than one kind, enabling the individual to carry just one card. At the simplest level, a

smart card for a transport system could cover rail, tram, bus and underground systems. A campus smart card could admit students to the campus area in the first place, act as a library card, a refectory account card, a campus shop debit card, and access card to secure areas such as computer laboratories.[5] More radically, services provided by more disparate organisations can be available from the same card – these are known as 'multi-functional cards'. Campus cards can be expanded from 'gown' to 'town' services, cards originally issued by transport companies could be platforms for health care, banking and other applications.

One-stop shopping
Smart cards could be used by consumers to reduce the transactions involved in using many services, through the creation of electronic 'one-stop shops', which may be on-line, to provide integrated service access points for, say, local government, or groups of related retail businesses.[6]

There are, of course, some risks for individuals as well. In much of the rest of this book, we examine the privacy risks. However, the simplest risk with cards is that they can be lost or stolen, and, if not 'locked', may be used by the finder or the thief. The more functions that are placed on the same card, the greater difficulties for the cardholder who loses her or his card. Again, with multi-functional cards, there are some minor technical complexities to be dealt with in cancelling a single application without affecting others.

Benefits for organisations
For government and business agencies that use personal data – 'data users', in the vocabulary of the Data Protection Act – smart cards also afford a number of benefits.

Security against fraud
Because a number of levels of security can be placed on and in the card, transactions can be far more secure than

those made manually or with magnetic stripe cards. Passwords, data encryption, error checking, and biometric information are all possible using smart cards – effectively eliminating the possibility of counterfeit cards.

A secure store of value
Electronic cash offers a measure of security that notes and coins cannot since data encryption and other security devices make the counterfeiting of this cash much more difficult than for banknotes.[7] Numerous security mechanisms render the forger almost entirely impotent. Even if a genuine card is stolen, the use of stored cash can be prevented: some electronic cash cards require the use of a PIN either to authorise the transfer of money into the cards, or to use during the transaction, while others (including the Mondex electronic purse) include a PIN to lock value on the card, which can be used when desired. If a true electronic cash card is lost, then, like lost notes and coins but unlike value accessed via a credit or debit card, the value cannot be refunded by the issuer.

Security against theft
The more electronic money is used, the fewer notes and coins will be kept in vulnerable retail tills, and at risk of physical theft by unsophisticated criminals.

Speedier transactions, especially off-line
As noted above, many transactions can also be conducted much more quickly, which can save organisations significant sums. Large savings for banks are also envisaged once the cumbersome use of cash is replaced by its more manageable electronic equivalent.[8]

Contactless cards could offer greater time savings. At present, most contactless cards are used to admit cardholder individuals to public transport systems, and the individual simply passes the card in front of the laser-powered reader device. However, the technology is capable of handling much richer information and more complex transactions more quickly.

A means of tracking consumer behaviour

Smart 'loyalty cards' issued by retailers mainly serve the function of enabling the retail company to track the purchases of the cardholder, in order to build up a profile of their consumer base, their preferences and interests (this, of course, is regarded by privacy activists as a risk for individuals). This is possible because the chip can be programmed to maintain an 'audit trail' listing transactions, including items, times, and sums involved over a period of time, which can be read by an authorised reader device. Alternatively, the smart card can provide an access key to a central database storing this information. (Some loyalty cards, such as the current Tesco card, are in fact magnetic stripe cards, and the information handling is done on a remote computer, but many retailers are opting for smart cards instead.)

Branding

The second and subsidiary function served by 'loyalty cards' – both smart and magnetic stripe cards – is essentially a marketing one. By physically branding the card with the logo of a brand, the card acts as a reminder 'advertisement' of the brand, and when it carries with it some entitlement to preferential treatment in discounts, interest free credit or other service, it can reinforce the consumer's willingness to purchase again.

Integration of related services

Smart cards can be used to integrate services into 'one-stop shops' which are cheaper and more convenient for businesses to run.

New charging systems

Smart cards may be the means by which new payment systems are created. For example, they may prove to be the most effective means to enable road pricing scheme to work.

Who is playing card games?

Take-up and take-off

Smart card technology is already a central part of the information age, and will become more so.

Although many technical advances are still awaited, innovative use of current smart card technology has become widespread, particularly within Europe. A wide range of applications has been developed in businesses and government services, and new applications are constantly emerging. Smart cards have proliferated rapidly, creating a dynamic and expanding market, estimated by one forecasting group to reach around £1.3 billion by the year 2000,[9] and predicted by another group to grow at an average annual rate of 41 per cent between 1993 and 1999.[10] The card-producing firm Gemplus have published the forecast of growth shown opposite.

Germany has introduced a national health insurance smart card. A new Spanish social security and health card is planned to provide quick access to vital information, promising to reduce both error and misuse. In some countries, the pressing need for secure forms of identification has been the crucial spur to wide business take-up. Banks across Russia, for instance, have introduced smart cards with fingerprint checks encoded

Fig.1 The growth in smart cards applications

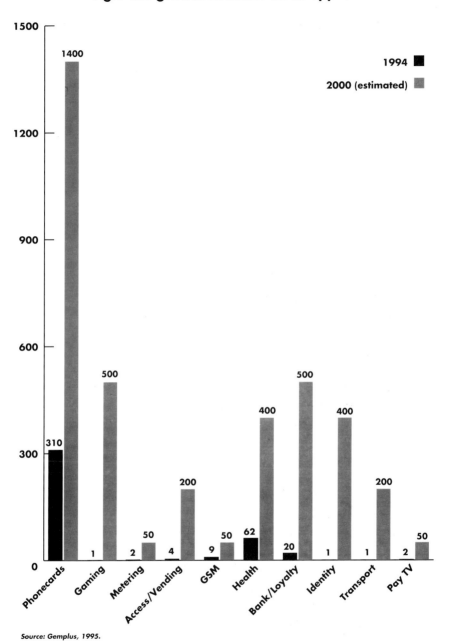

Source: Gemplus, 1995.

upon them. In South Africa, some employees withdraw their wages from cash machines which verify identity by comparing stored fingerprints with a reading of the fingerprint of the person presenting the card.[11]

Greater usage of smart cards in one nation, especially within the European single market, will rapidly spill over into others. The introduction of a rechargeable smart card by the German telecommunications giant Deutsche Telekom could prove a major influence. The chip in the card has a memory structure able to support the conversion between pre-paid currencies and it could act in addition as a banking card. Although the system is only operating at first in Germany, Deutsche Telekom hope that within several years the card may come to represent a de facto European or international standard phonecard.[12] Smart cards for international public transport, electronic cash or health cards in any major European country will also bring pressure for convergence in standards and international use of the technology.

Cards are now being used in applications as diverse as satellite television decryption and the tracking of peanut sales in the US,[13] but the greatest number of trials and applications has been for telecommunications, loyalty cards, electronic cash, health and transport. In these areas, three forms of use have evolved, each of which employs a different technical architecture and a different system for identification.

Functions
First, some cards *store monetary value* and have been employed in transport applications and other retail payment systems. These cards need not provide any form of identification, since, like the phonecards used in the UK, they can be bought anonymously with a ready store of value. Some cards can be re-loaded with additional value.

Second, cards carrying some form of *identification* and *personal information* are of greater interest to governments and businesses wishing to maintain secure access to their services, or needing a means to read reliable information about the individual. Health and loyalty cards clearly require these forms of application, and government identity cards, too, could have similar facilities for identification and information storage.

Third, in recent years, smart cards which *store value, authenticate the card and the card reading system, and yet do not store rich information about the individual cardholder* have become more widespread. Of these, Mondex is one of the best examples (although even here, a limited amount of personal information in the form of an audit trail – involving only the ten most recent transactions – is 'remembered' by the card; see below).

We now briefly review the most interesting developments in the key industries where smart cards are being used.

Financial services: 'electronic cash'

Of many smart card uses, the 'killer application' is widely believed to be electronic cash. Many other uses of card technology serve business interests first, and often benefit consumers in only marginal ways. Electronic cash, by contrast, offers immediate and tangible rewards to consumers from fast, secure transactions and on-line transfers of funds.

Many attempts have been made to develop cards capable of transferring funds from buyer to seller in the same way as cash. Previous card technologies, however, have consistently failed to guarantee against alteration of the information on the card, making it relatively easy to counterfeit currency (easily done on magnetic stripe cards).[14] The inclusion of a chip enables the introduction of the necessary level of protection. Smart card systems can incorporate security features, including cryptography and tamper resistance, to ensure that the monetary value on a card can only be exchanged within a valid system and cannot be added to without authorisation. As a result, a consumer now has the prospect of secure off-line payment of electronic cash into a reader device held by a retailer or even another individual.

Initiatives

In at least twenty-four countries across the globe, various forms of electronic cash and electronic purses are being developed and implemented. Electronic purses are being promoted on a nationwide basis in Portugal,[15] and pilot schemes are being run in Belgium, Austria and Denmark. From next year a national roll-out of electronic cash called 'Chipknip' is planned for the Netherlands[16] – involving cards storing up to 500 guilders of value – to complement two other planned national electronic purses. These various financial applications range from simple disposable cash cards, which discharge a bought store of value – like the Visa cash card, piloted in Australia and various US states – to electronic purses connected to bank accounts, to smart credit and debit cards.[17]

The Mondex pilot scheme in Swindon is one of the most technologically sophisticated of these electronic purse schemes. Mondex operates as a complete alternative to cash. Like cash, there is no need to check the identity of the person using the card; the authentication of the card itself is sufficient. Numerous security features and 'locking' devices make counterfeiting and other forms of fraud extremely arduous,[18] while the user has the maximum autonomy and freedom of use without intrusion. The card can already be loaded with value over the telephone,[19] and in future may be used as a payment mechanism in other areas, including the Internet.

Regulators such as the Bank of England are concerned by the possibility that smart cards could be used more easily for money laundering than traditional manual systems, because cards can handle very large sums that would attract suspicion in other forms. This is of particular concern as cards that operate in more than one currency are introduced. However, cash limits per card could be set, or other forms of electronic checking on sources might alert bankers to suspicious transactions.

Within Europe, the market for electronic purses is becoming steadily more competitive. Apart from the many national schemes mentioned above, three major card issuers – Europay, Visa and Mastercard – are engaged in uncomfortably strained negotiations aimed at setting down specifications for a smart credit card, and smart electronic purses.[20] Experts in the industry are convinced that these standards for electronic purses, due in June 1996, will establish a system for stored value in which every transaction is recorded and processed separately – by contrast with the much greater anonymity ensured in the Mondex system.

A major spur to the development of smart technologies in financial services will almost certainly be the emergence of a single European currency at least in a core group of states. European banks will need to create and operate payment systems in the Euro, as the currency is to be called. It is natural that they will want to begin with the construction of electronic payment systems, which are cheaper and faster to operate than traditional monetary technologies. Even banks based in countries outside the Euro zone will need to offer their business clients facilities for operations in the Euro, and will need to be part of the inter-bank payment systems that emerge. This could lead quickly to the emergence of consortia of banks offering international electronic Euro-cash or at least smart debit and credit cards denominated in Euros and perhaps other European currencies too.

Anonymous cash versus identified credit
Few banks which have experimented with electronic purses or cash appear at all enthusiastic about a complete 'hands-off' approach to electronic cash. Indeed, in almost all European schemes, the recording of transactions means the schemes are not strictly cash-like. For some banks, this is simply an issue of maintaining some regulatory control over monetary flows. But any electronic purse which processes all transactions also

provides card-issuers (like banks or credit firms) with the opportunity of extracting a processing charge on every exchange. Squeezing paper cash out of the market could thus lead to huge profits for issuers.

Mondex maintains a minimal audit trail, apparently both to safeguard the security of the system and to remind users of their recent purchases, but there is no permanent log of every transaction. The Dutch company, Digicash, has responded to concerns over the privacy of electronic cash systems by devising secure and anonymous systems of e-cash payment, both on smart cards and over the Internet.[21] Although this system of anonymous cash is still run by banks, and regulated by banking authorities, the bank cannot keep any tabs on the movement of cash within the economy, or trace who has made any particular transaction. As a result, a lost card cannot be returned to the consumer, nor can a dispute about short-changing be resolved. In other words, it is the purest form of electronic cash – warts and all. This method of completely anonymous payment is now being road-tested in Europe, and has already been brought to the market by the Mark Twain bank in the US.

Health care

Health care promises to be one of the most important and beneficial fields of use for smart card technology, yet one that unleashes the fiercest debates about privacy and misuse of personal information.[22]

Germany has implemented a national system of smart health cards with details of health insurance upon them (but no data about the cardholder's health),[23] while the French Vitale card, containing details of the cardholder's health insurance and prescription forms, has already been piloted in seven areas with the eventual intention of completely replacing paper prescriptions.[24] In the UK, the pilot Exmouth Health Care Card received very positive responses from both users and professionals alike.[25]

The central issues in the area of health revolve around the use to which the information is put. Storing information on a health card could provide straightforward access to health details for relevant officials, and could prove enormously helpful for emergency services. Any viable health card will need to be composed of multiple, separate directories, which can be read by relevant officials or professionals (pharmacists, doctors, ambulance workers, etc.). In one respect, this is simply a question of constructing a card architecture with secure 'firewalls' around each directory. This was achieved in the Quebec Health Card introduced in 1993, and also in the Ontario Encounter Card project conducted between 1992 and 1993.[26] Beyond this immediate and resolvable technological concern, there remain serious issues about the status of doctor-patient records (which are widely treated as confidential), the ownership of the data on the card, and the access of government or insurance companies to stored information, and to information from other applications that may be stored on multi-functional cards. For these reasons, health cards involve some of the most complex and stubborn conflicts of interest of all.[27]

Transport

Transport systems already make ready and effective use of smart cards, especially contactless cards. Cards can be charged with value and then re-charged once their value has been depleted. Already, this has enabled several public transport systems to integrate the technology into their operations. In Finland, for instance, smart cards are used for long-distance bus travel,[28] while London Transport is planning a smart card system to ease congestion at ticket booths and speed up passengers transit through tube stations. A similar system of smart cards based on payment for local transport operates in Greater Manchester, through the OneCard.[29] In due course, local public transport smart cards, with reliable bases of users – such as the 3.5 million expected to regularly use the card in London – may provide a base for multiple application cards tied into the services and retail outlets of a particular locality.

There is no necessity in current transport use of smart cards for any information about the individual to be encoded on the card. Indeed, the Hong Kong smart card ticketing system for all public transport allows users the choice of an anonymous system or a personalised card.[30] But as smart card use spreads into other forms of transport, the call for ready individual identification on the cards will become more pressing. By the end of the decade, it has been estimated that 50 per cent of the use of smart cards will be for transportation, either through payment systems for public transport, car entry systems (into private car parks, for instance), or toll collection systems on motorways.[31]

In most tolling systems, value is deducted from cards or other smart devices held in units in the car as the vehicle passes under a gantry. The main technical difficulty with these systems is that they are costly, because it takes a great deal of power to activate a card at a distance. These devices need not use the true identity of the driver or the owner of the car. But tolling could potentially involve billing of car users, and thus identification of the driver's name and address, combined with comprehensive listing of their exact movements. The potential privacy implications have been raised by the German media in connection with recent federal government schemes for road pricing.

Retail sector: 'loyalty cards'

As we have noted, for retailers, smart cards appear to offer advanced technology and the possibility of tying consumers into 'loyalty' schemes. Cards hold identification of the consumer, and an audit trail of purchases, enabling retailers to profile their consumers' behaviour and interests.

The simple 'loyalty' benefits of these schemes for retailers are uncertain. Loyalty in the marketplace is something of a phantom, and surveys in the USA have shown that the consumers holding the greatest number of loyalty cards are generally the most promiscuous in their shopping behaviour.[32] Apart from loyalty schemes, proprietary schemes run by utilities have also been developed, such as the British Gas Quantum Card, which transfers information on the consumer from the domestic meter to the utility.[33]

Telecommunications

At present telecommunications is the dominant sector in smart card issue and usage. Payphone smart cards, most of which are anonymous, account for around 80 per cent of all smart cards. Telecommunications may also well provide one of the basic smart card infrastructures of the future, upon which multiple application cards can be built. The Global Standard for Mobile Communications (GSM) – used in all European mobile phones, and adopted as a standard in many other countries – is realised in the physical form of a smart card which allows mobile phone subscribers to be identified and connected. Potentially this could be enhanced to provide a multi-functional card, and, in the longer term, a global standard for identification.

Other areas of commercial industry are now either planning to introduce or actively promoting smart cards for various purposes, ranging from loyalty cards to payment systems. These include pay-television, the utilities, and the retail petroleum industry.

Government and the public sector

As identity cards for citizens, smart cards raise the spectre of state surveillance of the individual. The British government's Green Paper of 1995 on identity cards suggested the smart card as one option, providing a ready source for identification, and a means for the citizen efficiently to make transactions and give vital information to all the various bodies in the public sector, including organisations dealing with health, benefits, education, and employment.[34]

Whether or not a single integrated card is introduced,

there are already a number of card-based initiatives taking place in a highly fragmented fashion within several government departments and agencies, including the Benefits Agency and the Driver and Vehicle Licensing Authority. However, none appears likely to introduce even a smart card system for their own purposes, since the costs of smart technology for a single application are high by comparison with the costs of magnetic stripe or other card technologies.[35] In other countries too, smart cards are still rarely used as identity cards, and where they have been introduced, it is with the provision of specific services in mind. One example is Spain, which has piloted a social security and health card, shortly to be implemented nationally. In the US, several states are experimenting with use of smart cards to store benefit payments. In Wyoming, for example, the state government is planning a multi-service card, and several other American states are planning to eliminate food stamps as coupons, by replacing them with electronic benefit transfer (EBT).[36]

Smart futures: drivers of change

The particular route by which smart cards become a nearly universal medium of identification and transaction is uncertain. Yet we can identify some key drivers of change, or trends in society and technology, which will shape the likely use of smart cards. We organise these forces into four clusters – those concerned with technical developments, those around the interests of issuers in business and government, trends in the regulation of cryptography, and those around the consumer interest. Naturally, these clusters are not completely distinct, and the interactions between them are often most important.

Technology
Card technology is developing rapidly:
- Smart cards are becoming cheaper.
- Multi-functional smart card technology is becoming more sophisticated: cards are now able to house separate directories and applications each with their own security mechanisms and encryption routines.
- Standards for multi-functional cards are being developed by a number of national and international bodies.

- All around the world, rapid progress is being made towards improving the capacity, speed and efficiency of the chips embedded in the cards.
- The development of contactless cards will further enhance possibilities for transport applications and secure entry into buildings.
- New 'super smart' cards, including a microprocessor, keyboard, liquid crystal display and power source, are now undergoing trials.[37]
- Chips that work both with contact and contactless reader devices are being developed.
- Improvements are being made in the security of encryption systems in all forms of communication and chip systems.

At present, there are still a number of serious brakes on rapid, universal deployment of smart cards. The main problem has arisen from the fragmented development of smart card schemes, almost all run by individual issuers in a proprietary fashion. Physical standards are in place for smart cards, covering physical dimensions, contact positions and the like, but there are as yet few common standards for data protocols or the operating systems – so that one palm-top reader device, for instance, could handle a number of rival cards with a variety of different applications using different architectures, encryption systems, etc. The technology is used by issuers for different applications, and consortia of companies are still rare.[38] Despite this fragmentation, standards for single and multi-functional applications are gradually starting to emerge for many services at the European level, including mobile phones, transport and health. But until these standards become universal, or one form of card achieves dominance, many companies will avoid investing heavily in smart card applications.[39]

Business demand
For business, loyalty schemes are prone to remain fragmented, because companies want to brand their own

cards. Consumers are unlikely to keep on acquiring ever more cards just for the opportunity of an occasional reduction in price, and loyalty schemes have limited track records of success in raising sales.

The greatest lure for the private sector will probably be the electronic purse. These systems promise to make shopping easier for the consumer, while also reducing the risk of false payment. Banks will also gain from the reduction in costs associated with handling cash, estimated to be as much as 1 per cent of gross national product.[40] A further potential attraction for businesses has also transpired in the Mondex pilot in Swindon, gathering some adverse publicity in the process. The Mondex card maintains a personal audit history of the last ten transactions, while large retailers will have the capacity via their Mondex reading machines to compile comprehensive trails of recent purchases, which can be mined over a period of days or weeks to compile personal purchasing histories. There are obvious limits to the usefulness of these data: the purchases are matched via the Mondex number, but the identity of the purchaser remains unknown to the retailer (since the name connected to the number is held by the bank in confidence).

Alternative systems, however, are less likely to be studiously cautious about the use or dissemination of individual identities. Most cash cards operate on the model of credit or debit cards, so that all transactions using electronic cash can be monitored and recorded on a central processing computer. Further protection against fraud and tighter identification procedures could even involve biometric identification of the individual and use of the cardholder's name. With the advent of new systems able to mine and match data more effectively, the benefits to companies of collecting transaction histories could be even greater than current loyalty cards can achieve, offering an electronic form of competitive advantage in a highly volatile and fluctuating retail marketplace.

In the field of telecommunications and loyalty

schemes, the progress of smart cards could start to undermine the clear distinction between money and other forms of goods. Telephone payment units are rapidly becoming the equivalent of cash in a world of fully electronic retail (as the executives of Deutsche Telekom seem to want). David Birch of the consultancy Hyperion has recently expressed his conviction that the difference between accumulated loyalty points such as air miles, and electronic cash, might start to become untenable.[41] Air miles could be exchanged for eggs, telephone units for bread, maybe even transport credit for cinema tickets. With common standard smart card architectures and international business co-operation, this possibility may not be too far distant, although the private issuing of electronic money based on business expansion programmes could, unless regulated carefully, prove highly inflationary.

Home shopping, purchasing over the Internet and total control systems for domestic appliances – one of the most beguiling applications in the information age – will make use of smart cards both as processors of information and keys for authentication. Satellite television in the UK already involves smart cards – with three million BSkyB cards currently being used as decryption devices – and pay-per-view television in the future may be expected to rely upon them. Telecommunications services make extensive use of smart cards in mobile phones, but we can expect card technology to become even more widespread once Personal Communications Networks (PCN) are created. In these systems, each subscriber could be allocated a unique telephone number at birth for use until death. Smart cards are the ideal means to identify users in such a system, regardless of the type of telephone they are using or their location.[42]

Government demand
Governments' employment of smart cards has thus far proceeded little further than use in health and social security. In these areas, smart cards are used as tokens to

prove entitlement, store personal information and track receipt of services. But it is the potential of smart cards as both a device to facilitate service provision and a form of identification that could prove most interesting for governments in the long term. One smart card with multiple directories could, in principle, replace the many cards we hold for identification purposes today, such as driving licences, health cards, or claimants' cards, while also allowing space for commercial identifications (video rental cards, shopping account cards) residing in the same chip.[43] Private and public services could operate through these smart cards, helping to streamline many government departments, while tapping into the many benefits smart cards can offer in the marketplace.

One recent paper arguing for a voluntary smart identity card, sponsored initially by the government but run by a private company under the Private Finance Initiative, contended that such a card would 'vastly enhance our efficiency and international competitiveness', and would 'represent a leap towards making Britain a true Information Society'.[44] The authors also envisage a smart card which improves the confidentiality of personal data through the encryption of data, strict separation of applications, and the opportunity for cardholders to read what is on their card files. The potential role of smart cards in the provision of front-line care services (for the elderly or disabled) has also been underlined.[45]

The administration of such a multi-functional government-issued card would almost certainly compel Whitehall departments, Next Steps agencies, health authorities and local authorities to co-ordinate their activities much more than ever before. Some people take the view that the intention behind the suggestion in the Green Paper on identity cards that a comprehensive smart identity card be issued, was that this would enable greater centralisation of personal information within central government. The Government Data Network is already a step further in this direction. While this would

43

certainly be a force for centralisation, some safeguards of access and privacy could be designed and put in place that would control or outweigh the risks to citizens from greater central power and efficiency in government. In the second half of this book, we offer some suggestions about what form those safeguards might take.

Regulation of cryptography

As we have seen, data on smart cards can be encrypted, or encoded for security. In principle, one might think, this might solve most of the problems about privacy. In practice, matters are not so simple. Governments around the world have made a variety of efforts to control the use of encryption by private individuals and companies. The extent to which encryption systems will provide security for the privacy of personal data on smart cards is therefore going to be determined partly by whether and how governments choose in future to regulate the use of strong cryptography.

Public and private key systems
The last thirty years have seen a revolution in techniques of cryptography, or the art of secure encoding of information to maintain secrecy and privacy.[46] A code is a key, or, in other words, an algorithm, or a mathematical procedure that transforms a piece of information systematically into a string of symbols – numbers, letters or other signs – that means nothing to someone who does not possess a key to reverse the procedure. In theory, any code can be cracked by 'brute force', or by searching all possible procedures until one is found that seems to work. In practice, modern cryptographic keys are so advanced that the computer power, time and resources required for such methods make them all but impracticable. Modern encryption systems are of various degrees of strength, depending not only on the mathematical complexity of the routine, but also on the 'size' of the key used, measured by the number of bits of information that make it up. The larger the key, the more difficult it is to crack

the code.

The major problem with traditional codes was that the sender had to find a way securely to give the recipient the key to 'unlock' the message. In the 1970s, a solution was found to this problem, known as 'public key encryption'. In such systems, everyone has two keys, a public key for encryption and a private key for decryption. The private key need never be exchanged. If a company wants to encode personal data on their client's smart card, they can use a publicly available key to do so: anyone would be able to encode additional information using that public key and perhaps, if the card's architecture permitted it, store it on a smart card issued by the company. However, the key needed to decrypt those data remains private, and only the company's own reader devices would be permitted to use it.

Provided the private key remains genuinely private, this system can be used in reverse as a way of authenticating the source of any information. Since only one company can encrypt a message using its own private key, anyone who decodes that information using the company's public key will know that the information could only have come from that company.

There is now a variety of public key encryption systems available relatively widely.[47] Many systems were developed either privately or within academic institutions or by commercial enterprises.

Prohibition and substitution policies
However, many government security and policing bodies regard the private use of strong cryptography with great disfavour. The argument has been that terrorists, enemy states, drug traffickers and others might use strong cryptography, and that in order to ensure that government code breakers are always capable of cracking the available codes, everyone should use a system which permits this. In short, what some governments fear is a scenario of 'too much privacy'.[48]

The United States government has long classified

cryptography along with weapons systems as a kind of military *matériel*, and has made various efforts, largely unsuccessful, to prevent its private use. Laws remain on the statute book in the US that prohibit the export of the stronger cryptographic systems. Individuals who have developed particular keys have been threatened with prosecution. The Clinton administration has pursued the strategy of developing an alternative system of encryption for use by individuals and companies, whereby government agencies would always hold a key for decryption of messages. It has sought to create a standard for a hardware implementation of its system, called the 'Clipper chip'. However, this initiative ran into a storm of protest, not only from the privacy lobby, but also from the computer industry which feared that it would be unable to sell computers overseas if customers believed that buying a US-built computer effectively put the FBI inside their information systems.[49]

Escrow
However, there are other regulatory alternatives. One option is called private 'key escrow'.[50] All users would 'escrow' their key to a trusted *private* registry or deposit house, which could be approved and regulated by government. Government law enforcement agencies would have to obtain a court order, on the basis that they had strong reason to believe that an individual or company, that had escrowed their keys there, was guilty of some crime and that only by gaining access to their key could vital evidence be gained, before they could require such a registry house to divulge a private key. The state of Utah, in its 1995 Digital Signatures Act, appears to be moving in this direction,[51] and Karlsruhe University has developed a smart card system with escrowed user keys.[52]

Such registries would have other uses in the information age, because they might smooth the way to the general use of smart cards. If such registries competed with each other on the basis that they took great care to accept only companies and individuals the trustworthiness, and respect for data protection principles, of which had been established by painstaking investigation, their 'stamp' on a trading company might be a powerful warranty for people concerned about their privacy.

Such registries might also provide emergency decryption should the company's own copy of its private key become corrupted, lost or damaged by hackers or by disgruntled employees on being sacked or made redundant, etc.

The question is whether such 'trusted third parties' will indeed be trusted, either by consumers, or by companies or indeed by government, and if governments insist that escrow registries are government agencies, whether the public will trust them to respect data protection principles any more than the companies or government agencies that escrow their keys to them.

In the UK, the Conservative government has expressed interest in escrow systems.[53] A Labour Party policy document is less attracted to key escrow, but suggest that judicial warrant should be required before law enforcement agencies should have the power to demand decryption.[54] However, neither has presented detailed policies. It is not yet clear, for example, whether in future, we can expect the Bank of England to demand that encryption systems for electronic cash cards be escrowed with the Bank, or privately, or not at all.

Regulatory policy on encryption will, therefore, shape the smart card market, because it could influence the trust that consumers and citizens place in data protection, perhaps the kinds of personal information that people will be willing to grant to companies, the capacity of suppliers of equipment and software to export their products, and the costs of doing business under escrow régimes.

Consumers
Most smart card development thus far have been driven primarily by the requirements of card issuers. This has led

to disparate and loosely connected card schemes in many areas.

However, if smart cards are to become indispensable in all our everyday routines, a closer match between the business or governmental benefits and improved services for the public has to be made. Certainly, the market in smart cards will not grow without a willing base of users. One recent survey indicated a latent interest in the use of smart cards in Britain: 57 per cent had heard of smart cards, and 61 per cent of these people regarded the cards as fairly secure.[55]

In the next chapter, we review in detail what is known of the present attitudes of consumers. However, for the present, we need note only that *on average* consumers show a wary pragmatism about smart cards, being willing to use them and provide information to companies and government bodies in return for specified benefits, subject to clear, adequate and enforced safeguards.

Certainly, public demand for easier and faster transactions, whether through credit, banking by phone, remote shopping or electronic cash, will require handing over more information to the companies involved. If the anonymity of the consumer is increased by the use of communications technologies, forms of secure identification to compensate are needed. Smart cards will be one of these mechanisms.

A favourable reception in all areas is not guaranteed. Most people would like to prevent certain sorts of information about themselves, such as health details, from ending up in the hands of certain corporate or government users. Furthermore, where no noticeable benefit is received in return, resistance might be very high.

From the viewpoint of the consumer, most smart card applications need hold few terrors. Indeed the first reported concern of consumers involved in smart card pilots has not been privacy, but rather prices and fears about the consequences of the loss of their card.[56] Yet if smart cards are to be accepted by consumers for an array of applications, a balance between the issuers' needs for information and identification, and the concerns of the individual, must be acknowledged and achieved. This is where government policy on data protection and smart cards can play a significant role; without it, smart cards might expand in scope over all parts of society and the economy, yet steadily undermine connections of trust in the process.

Taking these drivers of change together, we can expect that the market will be divided between three types of smart cards – single application, multi-functional cards controlled by issuers, and multi-functional cards controlled by consumers. Depending on the relative strength of the forces discussed above, one of these types may become dominant.

Single application cards

The single application card is the most commonly available today. Branded by one organisation, it encompasses a single service or at most services provided by one organisation.

Issuers may prefer them, because they fear that their marketing and branding strategies may be undermined by allowing their application to co-reside with others, or if they fear that other organisations might produce applications that would 'interfere' with theirs, either by reading their data or altering it. Consumers might prefer single application cards, if they are very concerned about privacy and fear that organisations might use the multi-functional card to read data intended for others, or if they are worried about the risks of losing a card that brings together a whole series of entitlements: privacy campaigners sometimes argue that fragmentation provides some protection.

Issuer consortium-controlled multi-functional cards

Where both issuers and consumers overcome their problems about trust and privacy, where the risks of loss of cards can be minimised effectively and where marketing can be effective without physical branding, we will see consortia of public and private bodies combine to issue jointly owned smart cards with several applications. The CAFE (Conditional Access for Europe) Card is one example of the progress in this direction, a multi-functional card being developed by companies and research institutes, with the help of the European Commission.[57] A similar project is being undertaken in Denmark, with the Danmønt electronic purse scheme.[58]

Issuers may prefer them for several reasons. Sharing the costs of investment and dissemination also shares risks. Lead investors can recoup costs by leasing or franchising space on the chip on their cards to other participants. Sharing basic identifier technology may also prove more cost-efficient than each organisation producing its own.

The government-issued identity card suggested as one option in the Home Office consultation paper of 1995 would be, if it were ever to be issued, in essence controlled by a consortium of government issuers.

Consumers too might prefer them for reasons of convenience, mainly because they may want to reduce the numbers of cards they carry around with them.

Consumer-controlled multi-functional cards

More radically, it is possible that a generation of cards will be issued, where the consumer decides just which applications to combine on which of their cards, just as a computer user might decide which files to combine on a floppy disk or a music lover might make up a compilation tape of music to listen to in the car. When offered a new smart card by, say, a local library, the consumer could decline, but present another card on which there is sufficient space in the memory, and ask the library to place their application on it. Consumers would probably have to make backups of their applications regularly, and could then move them around at will, to ensure that even if they lost one card with several applications on it, they would have a backup that they could draw on, and have validated and perhaps updated in a single on-line transaction. Such consumer-controlled multi-functional cards would probably have to be owned by the consumer rather than by the issuers. Naturally, the more sophisticated consumers would be the first to take up such cards. However, the fact that many consumers are not sophisticated is not a reason for consumer-controlled cards not to be introduced, any more than it is a reason for not introducing any sophisticated product the use of which carries some risks.

Trust and the politics of privacy

The information society, risk and privacy

Smart cards are only one part of a wider spread of electronic information gathering and communication technologies which will change many relations between individuals, business and the state. So what exactly will an 'information society' involve, and what sort of consequences might it have for the power and freedom of the citizen?

At the launch of the plan for a National Information Infrastructure in 1993, US Vice-President Al Gore invoked the vision of a 'seamless web' of interconnecting networks, databases and computers which could provided unlimited access to enormous stores of learning and entertainment.[59] Such an information society and economy will be based around smart cards, networks, powerful desk-top computing and multimedia communications. Although only one part of a web of technologies, smart cards are set to become a central means through which information is acquired and transacted, products bought, and identities verified. This is certainly a glowing vision, but alongside optimism it brings new challenges and risks.

One significant consequence could be fewer face-to-face

encounters with shopkeepers or government officials, as much of the citizen's business is conducted electronically, and a more impersonal relationship between individuals and large organisations. Secondly, the central role of smart information technologies in individuals' dealings with government and business – largely as result of the need to compensate for more impersonal relations between these individuals and organisations – generates concerns over privacy and intrusiveness into citizens' lives. The fear is that smart cards could become 'Big Brother's little electronic helpers',[60] contributing an extra layer of potential surveillance, in addition to the new prying capacities of interactive media and satellite.[61] Thirdly, proposals in the UK for government-issued smart identity cards could change the British scene radically and rapidly. As multi-functional cards appear in the next ten years, some of these concerns will become sharper. We detail the nature of these fears and the likelihood of their being realised in the next three chapters.

Alternatively, smart cards can be used as a tool for enhancing security and anonymity. They need not contain identification about the individual, and even if they contain card identification, the connection between this and the individual could remain confidential. For example, this is the case with the Mondex electronic cash card. The processing power of the chip on a smart card allows it to store information, which could enable a greater distribution of information as opposed to a centralisation. Certainly, the information will have to be correspondingly filed in a central system, but it might be possible to store this information anonymously, to be retrieved by use of a PIN or a biometric identifier. Only information on the card could straightforwardly be attached to an individual.

Indeed, since smart cards are carried – although not usually owned – by the person to whom they apply, information could in principle be more effectively monitored by the citizen.

Whether these cards work to undermine or to buttress

privacy, it is clear that the gains in convenience, efficiency, security and economic growth that smart technologies promise will be realised only if the public trust the government agencies and businesses that offer them cards. We now review what is known about public attitudes and then proceed to consider the rival arguments of business people and technologists on the one hand, and civil libertarians on the other, about how real the risks to privacy from smart information technologies are.

Public fears

At present, a large proportion of the public, as consumers and as citizens, do not feel particularly trusting, either in government or business generally or, more specifically, in their willingness to design systems that will respect privacy and confidentiality of personal information.

Consider, first, the public's general suspicion about organisations that will offer them smart cards. Surveys by the Henley Centre for Forecasting and Gallup show that over the last decade and more, people report falling confidence in a wide range of public and private organisations. (See Figure 2 opposite).

People generally express more trust in service-providers such as doctors and pharmacists, with whom they have face-to-face contact, where the service is delivered by an identifiable individual rather than a large organisation, and where they believe that individual is subject to a code of professional ethics that puts the consumers' interest first.

It follows that if smart technologies are the harbingers of a more faceless way that individuals will deal with big organisations in general, then they will presumably only erode trust.

Secondly, much of the public seems to have quite sophisticated and discriminating views on which organisations hold personal information about them as individuals – probably on the basis of being asked to provide it – and to which sorts of organisations they feel

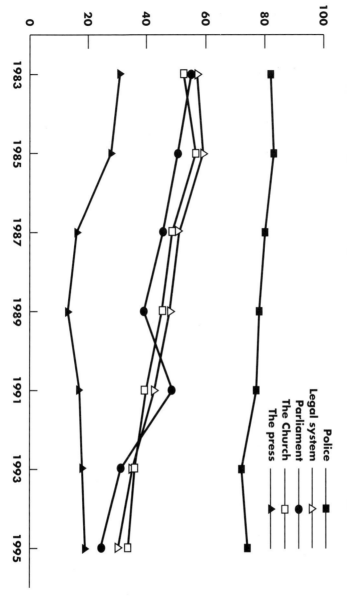

Fig.2 Dramatic fall in confidence in national institutions

% who have a great deal or quite a lot of confidence in the following...

Police	■
Legal system	▷
Parliament	●
The Church	□
The press	▶

Source: The Henley Centre/Gallup

Fig.3 The gap: who has and who could have information about you

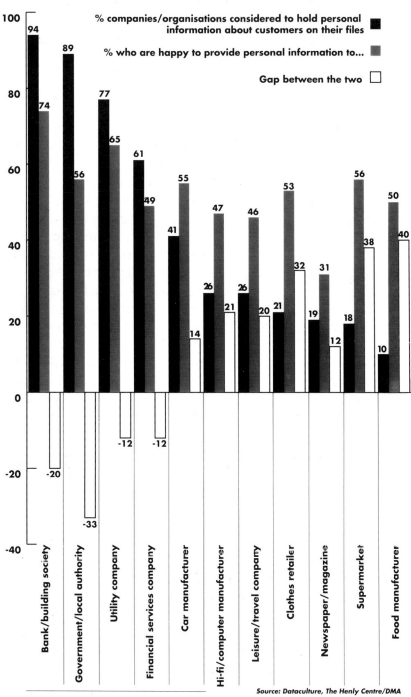

% companies/organisations considered to hold personal information about customers on their files

% who are happy to provide personal information to...

Gap between the two

Source: Dataculture, The Henly Centre/DMA

happiest in providing that information, about what sort of information they are willing to provide, and on what terms.

The Henley Centre and the Direct Marketing Association's survey for the Henley Centre report, *Dataculture*, identifies clearly that the 'gap' between feeling content to provide personal information to an organisation and knowing that in practice that organisation holds such information is greatest in the case of public sector organisations. Simply, they find that we trust government less than we trust business of any kind with the most intimate facts about our lives. (See Figure 3).

Most important for policy-makers, the same survey also found that people believe that large numbers of businesses do not comply with the data protection laws. If they lack confidence in the effectiveness of the systems of regulation in disciplining business, they probably have even less confidence that public sector agencies comply.

Other research suggests that this picture is too crude, and that people place different degrees of trust and distrust in different kinds of public sector agencies. For example, survey research commissioned by the Office of the Data Protection Registrar suggests that the National Health Service is highly trusted to respect data protection principles, while the police and the Inland Revenue are much less trusted. (See Figure 4 overleaf).

A similar partial ranking of the degree of trust in public and private agencies to respect confidentiality of personal information is also suggested by the US Harris Equifax survey 1994, which found 44 per cent of the American public had doubts about health insurers, while only 22 per cent worried about colleges and universities.[62]

The Henley Centre survey asked people what information people were willing to provide to companies. Ranking the percentages of those willing to give each type yields a hierarchy of types of information, and we can think of those types which the fewest people would be prepared to give as that which the public considers most personal. (See Figure 5 overleaf).

Fig.4 Members of the public were asked to say how satisfied they were that various organisations can be trusted to keep and use information in a responsible way

	1989 %		1990 %		1991 %		1992 %
Doctors and the NHS							
Satisfied	90		88		91		92
Not satisfied	4		5		5		5
Banks and building societies							
Satisfied	83		80		83	*	78
Not satisfied	9		11		10		13
Employers							
Satisfied	72		71		75		74
Not satisfied	12		11		10		11
Police							
Satisfied	72		71		69		72
Not satisfied	18		14	*	20	*	15
Inland Revenue							
Satisfied	66	*	60	*	66		68
Not satisfied	19		19		19		17
Schools and colleges							
Satisfied	61		61		65		66
Not satisfied	15		11		12		12
DHSS							
Satisfied	59		58		61		63
Not satisfied	22		20		18		16
Shops and stores							
Satisfied	31		33		35		36
Not satisfied	43	*	32	*	39		41
Credit reference agencies							
Satisfied	27		26	*	31	*	25
Not satisfied	47		44		44		49
Mail order companies							
Satisfied	25		21		23		23
Not satisfied	55		49	**	53	**	57

* = statistically significant over a two year period.
** = statistically significant over a one year period.

Source: Extract from Eighth Report of the Data Protection Registrar July 1992

Fig.5 The hierarchy of personal information

Not very personal

Family structure
Gender (but Miss, Mrs, Ms a problem for some)
Hobbies/lifestyle
Shopping/spending patterns
TV viewing
Car ownership
Appearance (hair colour etc)

Personality
Newspaper readership
Telephone number
Educational background
Politics/religion
Medical history
Income

Very personal

What personal details are you prepared to give to company if requested?

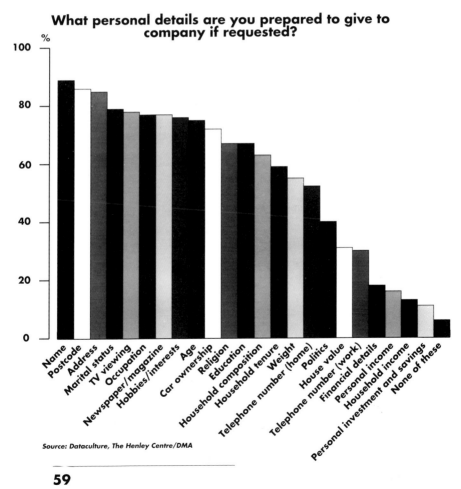

Source: Dataculture, The Henley Centre/DMA

Only about 9 per cent were unwilling to give organisations any information about themselves at all, and could be regarded as 'privacy fundamentalists'; on the other hand, only about 8 per cent had no worries whatsoever. Four out of five people are anxiously pragmatic, willing to give information about themselves in return for services but concerned about the weakness of the safeguards.

Moreover, the Henley Centre survey found people want a measure of control over how organisations acquire information about them. The public is aware that organisations can often acquire information about individuals by buying it or persuading another organisation to pass it on, and may even think it inevitable that this will sometimes happen. Few people have much confidence in the security of electronic databases either from hackers or from access approved by the organisations that hold the information. However, they dislike this behaviour, because they have no control over the accuracy or the use of the information, or who can gain access to it.[63]

Reassurance from business and technology inter interests

When confronted with such fears, professionals and insiders in the privacy and technology debate tend to react in one of two ways.

Business people working in direct marketing or in technology development often tend to be dismissive. Their arguments are threefold.

First, it is claimed such fears as irrational or even paranoid. They argue that, whatever the motives of government, business at least has no commercial reasons for behaving like Big Brother. Competitive pressures lead businesses to demand only quite narrow ranges of information about people, and the need to retain the loyalty of consumers who can easily go elsewhere will discipline those few companies that go too far. If what consumers want is a measure of security, and even anonymity, then those companies that provide services in those ways will have the edge.

They sometimes go on to argue that it is only government, which must exercise coercive power over citizens, that has any reason to override privacy, and in that case, its powers to do so are often circumscribed by other rules, such as police powers legislation.

Second, they would argue, modern information technology offers greater security against unauthorised access than anything previously available. With
● biometric authentication systems using electronic imprints from the thumb or the retina that cannot be counterfeited,
● password routines,
● encryption of sensitive data including passwords and biometric records using systems that have given the advantage to the encrypter over the would-be decrypter,
● the possibility that only access keys to centrally stored and protected databases will be kept in cards,
● the availability of 'pseudo-identifiers' that give anonymity when it is wanted,
information systems can now be more secure than any paper-based system or traditional database ever could be.

Third, they suggest, market research for most smart technologies suggests that people's fears about privacy are much less significant than one would think from the surveys we have cited. In fact, they suggest, privacy is hardly ever mentioned spontaneously by consumers and potential consumers: they have to be prompted to raise it. Much more important concerns spontaneously raised are about the consequences for the service if they should lose their card: will there be any way, consumers worry, to establish my entitlement to the service, or to the value stored on the card, if I have lost it?

Moreover, the business argument runs, most people know full well that complete privacy is impossible and are largely resigned to the fact. There never has been since the dawn of modernity, they argue, a golden age when privacy was possible.[64] Public opinion, they suggest, is ahead of the civil libertarians and the privacy lobby, in accepting that the benefits in services offered by the information society outweigh any loss of privacy. (Taken to its extreme, of course, this argument is not entirely consistent with the second one.)

The civil libertarian case

Civil libertarians, on the other hand, respond by arguing that the public are right to fear the abuse of confidential data both by government and by business, for the safeguards are, they say, far too weak.

Types of information
Fears have been expressed at one time or another by privacy specialists and by campaigners about the possibilities that any of the following kinds of information might be accessible from smart cards, whether stored in the card or reachable on central databases for which the card contains access keys, and that unauthorised individuals or organisations might obtain them:
- immigration status;
- previous convictions, including 'spent' convictions;
- religion;
- ethnic or tribal or racial or linguistic group;
- health status (e.g. HIV status);
- health-related personal behaviour (e.g. smoking, drinking, recreational drug use);
- sexual orientation;
- educational achievement;
- mental health status;
- social worker's views on character or fitness as a parent
- tax status;
- police opinions or suspicions about criminal involvement or connections with people believed to be involved in crime;
- income and wealth;
- credit rating;
- history of purchasing or consuming certain goods and

services (including titles of books borrowed from public libraries).

Organisations could use any of these types of information to draw inferences about an individual and, in consequence, deny services unfairly.[65] Of course, there are many situations where it will be advantageous to the individual that someone else should know these characteristics. But because there are many where it could lead to unfair treatment, individuals ought, the civil libertarians will argue, to have as much control as possible over the creation and use of personal information records about themselves.

Business and government motives
Civil libertarians do not accept the argument that business has no commercial reason to behave like Big Brother. Businesses need to know ever more about their consumers, in order to design products to appeal to them, to identify the characteristics statistically associated with a desire for the products they produce, or else to sell on to other businesses that use such information. This is the main purpose of the loyalty card. Indeed, some supermarket chains are experimenting with surveillance systems that collect information in great detail about how shoppers move around stores, what they stop and look at, what they put back, and so on: similar tracking systems are being developed for users of some electronic page systems. While not all of this information may be digitally stored and logged against an identified individual shopper, these developments show clearly the extent of businesses' commercial reasons for wanting to obtain large amounts of personal information.

Government's interest in general surveillance is well known, for reasons of maintaining national security, detecting criminals, collecting taxes and determining who is eligible for public services.

To the technologists' claim that password and encryption systems make smart data technologies secure, they reply that decryption keys can be passed between government departments, bought and sold by businesses, or acquired by industrial espionage. Any technology, they say, is only as secure as those who use it are willing to allow it to be.

Concern and awareness

When businesses argue that few people report privacy concerns in their market research, civil libertarians reply that this is because most people are not aware of the risks, but that when they are made aware, they report much higher levels of concern about privacy. Some qualitative research commissioned by the Office of the Data Protection Registrar strongly suggests that privacy concerns are latent but significant in this way.[66]

Abuses

It is quite possible, they argue, that personal information that is either stored on smart cards or that can be obtained by reading and using the access keys held on cards to central databases, may be

● written to the card or central database, collected, read, used, matched with other data from other sources, passed on, manipulated, compared with personal information about other individuals, all without the knowledge or the express or implicit consent of the individual concerned to any of these transactions;

● known or shown to the individual only in part, or in a misleading form or context;

● inaccurate, or just plain false;

● not factual in character and irrelevant to the legitimate purpose for which the organisation has the right to access information electronically stored – for example, information about a doctor's or a social worker's or other official's opinion of the individual's character;

● true, but inappropriate for the legitimate purposes for which the organisation has access rights to personal data – such as a record of a person's religion or sexual orientation or reading matter; or

● true and appropriate to the legitimate purposes of the organisation, but which the law or the contract between the individual and the organisation would normally prevent the organisation from having the right to know, because current public policy is that risks should be borne by the organisation and not the individual – such as details of someone's 'spent' previous convictions.

Data matching and data mining
Alongside the rich and varied forms of communication which will become instantly accessible to users of the 'information superhighway' will be mines of information about these very individuals. At present, information is stored in central databases by a great number of institutions, such as banks, government departments, health services, the police, retailers, credit card companies, schools, universities and libraries. That so much personal information is held on cards and databases and that networks support cross-referencing, often without the knowledge of the data subject, much more readily gives rise to greater risks, or at least to understandable fears.

There are concerns about inspection by unauthorised organisations. Indeed, authorisation procedures in British law are not particularly onerous, by comparison with, for example, Australian law which places clear time limits, requires that extraneous data be deleted after matching and insists that a formal application for permission be made in advance.

Information from, say, health records, transaction histories, and even library records can much more easily be combined to form personal profiles. This 'data matching', using individual and card identifiers and 'recombinant data'[67] in constructing character portraits can lead to error or at least the creation of misleading information, which is then used – again without the individual's knowledge – by government departments or businesses in decisions about how individuals are treated.

Of course, such data matching is already being done by

business and government, using existing methods of on-line connection. Some 80 per cent of Americans now inform pollsters that they are concerned about their total loss of control over personal information.[68] Smart cards merely represent an additional layer of information storage. But the real increased risk from smart cards arises from the frequency of their use. They could well become so ubiquitous, and so necessary for the acquisition of goods using electronic cash, travel, and in transactions with government departments, that a citizen's entire life is charted and stored. Numerous cases of data abuse have arisen since the 1960s, when central databases first started to become commonplace.[69] As information increases in depth and quantity, and its recombination is multiplied, the threat becomes even greater. While the 1984 Data Protection Act does give the Registrar powers to act in these cases, these powers are not very extensive.

Perhaps few people are directly harmed by these mines of data, but the mere presence of such information has been widely taken to be an infringement of personal freedom and the power of self-determination. If we do not know what large organisations know of us and when they know it, our ability independently to determine our fate may be eroded.[70]

Function creep
The very existence of large quantities of personal information, electronically available whether over networks from central databases or from smart cards using reader devices, will, both privacy regulators and civil libertarians argue, lead to its abuse. Once the infrastructure of smart cards and reader devices is in place, 'function creep' will occur: new roles and expectations will be placed on the cards, and information collected for one purpose will be used for others. This is most likely where the market is dominated by issuer-controlled multi-functional smart cards that are rich in personal data, and used mainly for off-line transactions,

rather than where they hold little more than access keys to on-line services. In these scenarios, reader devices will emerge that will secure access to the full range of information in cards. It could gradually become accepted as normal that insurers and employers will demand access to all the data held in cards at the point someone applies for cover or for a job: privacy regulators are already dealing with such cases.[71]

Radical views
For some radical civil libertarians a smart identity card, whether voluntary or compulsory, and even with rights for the cardholder to read the data, would still constitute a significant interference with personal privacy. One of the grounds for their suspicion of smart cards is that their issue is rarely, if ever, the result of demand by citizens or consumers. In other words, they are issuer-driven. This is one reason why those who suspect the motives or the power over individuals of many of the organisations that issue cards also distrust the implications of the technology for rights to privacy. A number of commentators, concerned by the threats to privacy and freedom from different quarters, have documented the historic and economic rationale for these technologies. In its most apocalyptic form, these new information gathering systems are seen as constituent parts of 'corporate society in a late stage of capitalist economic development'.[72] States and corporations, in this version of events, inevitably seek to control markets and individuals. Smart cards are just one manifestation of this; huge and detailed databases and closed-circuit television are others. All these things are seen by this radical group as part of the endless search for control by businesses and government in a disorderly and chaotic world.

Balancing risk and reason
Both the sanguine emollience of the business technologists and the alarmism of the civil libertarians

are probably misplaced, but both make important points.

The limits of libertarianism

The jeremiads of the traditional extreme civil libertarians fail to understand much of the new technology. In particular, they fail to recognise the shift in power that the new encryption systems give to the coder, the extent to which the hacker is now the one at a disadvantage, and the possibilities for privacy-enhancing technologies. (There are of course radicals who are more sophisticated and have great hopes of cryptography as a source of privacy.[73]) They also tend to ignore the variety of motivations behind the use of smart card technology. But perhaps they are right to point out that the needs and strategies of big social institutions are likely to dominate much development in the smart card market. Whether this leads directly to greater levels of intrusion depends on how the cards are developed and what policies are adopted in response.

It is important to distinguish within the arguments of the civil libertarians those concerns that are about data confidentiality, and those which are really about wider issues of social policy and the distribution of risks and burdens that may arise from the formal granting of rights of access to particular kinds of personal information. For example, someone who objects to insurers and employers having access to, say, genetic information about people applying for cover or for a job, is making a larger claim than one simply about the right of privacy. For, if insurers and employers are to be denied the right to such information, then social responsibility for bearing certain risks is being transferred. In the case of insurance, a regulation that required insurers to grant or deny cover to individuals in the absence of knowledge about their genetic risk of contracting certain diseases, in effect mandates risk pooling between individuals with low and high risks. In the case of hiring decisions, a similar rule would lay the burden on the employer of the risk of hiring someone who contracts a long-term illness.

This would be a major piece of paternalist intervention. In this book, we cannot deal with these issues, because they go far beyond concerns about access to personal information, restricting information to that which is relevant, etc.

Real risks of abuse
The idea that the market will always benefit companies that respect privacy is not wholly credible, precisely because consumers cannot know which companies do and which do not, and so cannot make an informed choice. A society, in which so much information can be obtained about individuals without their knowing, is one in which market mechanisms will not be sufficient to ensure respect for the general principles of data confidentiality. Some additional form of regulation is required to make the market deliver that.

To be sure, where there is competition and where the information that companies need about their consumers' behaviour is not particularly intrusive or not particularly likely to lead to adverse decisions about how consumers should be treated, the market may work tolerably well. Respectable companies that show themselves trustworthy will then have an advantage.

There is a role for self-regulation and the development of codes of practice. The Office of the Data Protection Registrar has played a part in encouraging self-regulation, and the new European Directive also seeks to promote them, but such codes are more widespread outside Britain.[74]

It is in those areas where what business does resembles government most, that a problem arises. Where there is little or no practical choice whether to consume the service – as in the case of having a bank account – limited choice of issuer, and great discretion for the issuer about what level of service if any to provide a given individual, consumers' experience is one of being *subjects*.

In such markets, the temptation for companies to seek access to more personal information will be very great.

Certainly, technologies are available that ensure anonymity for most of the time in such markets. For example, the holder of a Mondex electronic purse is, in normal use, anonymous to the Mondex reader device in use by a retailer, and rather extraordinary efforts and technological sophistication would be needed for someone to identify a person from brief access to their Mondex card. However, many banks and other institutions prefer less anonymous and less cash-like forms of electronic money, with a corresponding reduction in the security of personal information and growth in potential intrusiveness.

The problems of multi-functionality

The concerns of the civil libertarians are more likely to be realised where people carry multi-functional smart cards, in which several applications created by different organisations co-reside. Such cards could lead to greater privacy abuses in several ways. They could become the platform for greater information sharing between organisations, especially if they are inscribed in some form or other with a single identifier, such as a number. Even if organisations abstain from sharing data, the fact that they are reading from the same card gives them the physical opportunity, should they wish to take it and if they can overcome the password and encryption hurdles, of peeping into data held by the others. It seems almost impossible to envisage any enforceable way to detect and penalise this using traditional methods.

Some of the more anxious potential users may eschew multi-functional cards for these reasons, and to that extent, the problem may be less serious. Nevertheless, there are already examples of multi-functional cards. In Germany already, banks and other companies offer a joint smart card on which a collection of logos appear. Clearly, relying on the business case for single application cards is not enough to allay the fears about privacy.

Practical business people usually point out here that, in many cases, if they want information about their clients and consumers, it may well in practice be quite possible to use other methods to find it. Moreover, those methods will, at the moment, usually be cheaper than 'hacking' into or buying the decryption keys for some other organisation's application on a jointly used smart card. However, this may not always be the case.

Secondly, the civil libertarians' fears have some greater justification in the case of contactless cards that hold access to rich personal data. In the early 1990s, most contactless smart cards probably hold access to very limited data, because their main application is in public transport, with subsidiary uses in granting physical admission through gates, doors and passageways into areas of buildings or zones of land in highly secure use. However, there are scenarios in which multi-functional contactless cards come into use, and could be read from powerful reader devices at a distance when the cardholder passes within range. It is not certain that encryption and other security arrangements would always suffice to prevent privacy being breached. At present, of course, such reader devices would be very power-hungry and difficult to use in any targeted way. Road pricing systems using overhead-gantry-based devices that read a vehicle-based smart card are perhaps the first stage, although many such systems planned at present would use single application cards and could be anonymous. As the technology develops, perhaps to include cards that can be read both by contact and contactless reader devices, and as people become used to multi-functional cards, this might change.

The value of privacy and the public trust
Business people and technologists are probably correct in saying that in the twentieth century and certainly in the information society of the next century, one would have to go to quite extraordinary lengths and eschew most of the benefits of modern life to achieve privacy. Most people are, as the Henley Centre survey showed, realistic about this.

It does not follow, however, that privacy will gradually cease to be an important value. Rather, it suggests that we need to think more carefully about the exact degree to which privacy which can be secured, and about which tools of public policy could be used for this purpose. We should also consider what citizens and consumers can expect to gain in compensation for the steady erosion of privacy. It is probably true that, until recently, it was the relative inefficiency in their information management capacities of most governments and companies that afforded much of the available space for privacy. Yet, if privacy is something of value, then it ought not to subsist hand-to-mouth in the interstices of the social order, but be underpinned both formally and organisationally in some way.

Even though Big Brother may not be watching, the public are surely right to be distrustful of companies and government sector agencies. Of course, most businesses are honest and would rather have the confidence of their consumers and most government is routine-bound, too concerned with regular processing to be inquisitive about citizens. Yet the facts that new techniques of data matching and data mining are available and that so much more information is potentially available about individuals will from time to time create risks that rightly worry people.

Clearly, many people fear the privacy implications of the new smart technologies, and they will in many cases be reluctant to accept smart cards for precisely that reason. True, smart cards may be no less secure than other systems, and it may even be likely that cards will typically use technologies that will provide some privacy protection. There is probably nothing intrinsically insecure about the technology that it should attract concerns about privacy. Yet business and government must address consumers and citizens as they find them. In a society that claims both to be a democracy and to enjoy a consumer-oriented service business culture, they are entitled to expect nothing less.

A case of mistaken identity? A government card

The consultation paper

On 24th May 1995, Michael Howard, Home Secretary, published his green paper, *Identity cards: a consultation paper*, which set out various options for a government-issued identity card.

Alternative choices included a paper card, a magnetic stripe card or a smart card; a card that combined the driving licence, passport, national insurance number, social security records, NHS health records, criminal record and the full range of information used by central government departments; some, all or none of these; a 'bare' identity card, or some reduced range of government data; a voluntary or a compulsory card; a card with extensive data stored in the chip, or a card with access keys for on-line transactions with centrally held government databases; a card with biometric identification capacity or one with a simple unique identifier.

It is certainly true that many services that government provides us with would be more conveniently conducted if the information involved were transacted using a card and perhaps on-line transactions as well.

The debate

Most of the concerns of the civil libertarians in the previous chapter were raised in objection, not only by civil liberties groups but also by Conservative politicians. It was pointed out that some of the choices were not real. Firstly, a 'voluntary' card would quickly become de facto compulsory, even if there was no actual duty to produce it and no powers for the police or the courts to draw inferences from non-possession or refusal to produce it.[75]

Government's assertions that uses of the card by the police would be benign and that 'honest people would have nothing to hide' were widely dismissed. Critics pointed to examples from other countries, where cards have been the basis of mistaken identity or have been used in a highly discriminatory manner.[76] The capacity of British government and police to use cards in a way that would not be unfairly discriminatory was widely questioned:[77] would black British people be asked to produce them more often that white, because of concerns about illegal immigration by Africans and Asians?

Some of the government's claims for the card hardly withstood scrutiny. The idea that it would help reduce social security fraud was undermined by the admission by Peter Lilley, Secretary of State for Social Security, that less than 5 per cent of such cases involved impersonation or identity errors. It seemed unlikely that forged cards would be so obvious to casual inspection at airports and seaports that illegal immigration would be reduced. Many of the police claims that detection rates would improve foundered on the fact that identity problems are not a very significant reason for failure to bring prosecutions or to make them stick, and in those cases where that is the issue, it is far from clear that the card would help.[78]

However, the main concerns were around privacy and state surveillance. Data in the cards, unless heavily protected, might be read and used by departments with interest in the information, even if it was explicitly provided for another reason: for example, health records might be used in the assessment of benefits claims. These data would also be stored by central government departments on their own systems, since the card must be replaceable in the event of loss or damage.

Data-matching techniques then give the state opportunities to amass comprehensive personal profiles, to be used when they see fit by all departments and private organisations working under contract to government to provide public services. The additional threat of this information being extracted from government databases by computer hacking or theft compounds this intrusiveness.[79]

A compilation of responses to the Green Paper was presented to the House Select Committee on Home Affairs in January 1996. Approximately 65 per cent of those respondents who had a view were in favour of some form of identity card, although they were split between support for a voluntary or compulsory card.

At present, it appears highly unlikely than any smart identity card scheme will be put forward before the next election; at most, a simple embossed plastic card, possibly with a magnetic stripe, might be proposed. The government will in all likelihood take its final decision following the release of the Select Committee's report on identity cards later in 1996. Some commitment to a 'voluntary' identity card scheme is widely expected to appear in the Conservative Party's next general election manifesto.

The odd feature of the whole debate was that both sides ignored the fact that Britons already carry any number of tokens which can be used as identity cards. The first function of most credit or debit cards, 'loyalty' cards, and others is to link a person's identity or account number with a service, and where they carry a photograph or other biometric, to ensure that the cardholder is the person with that identity. For purely identification purposes, most of us already carry a choice of identity cards, and there is no evident need for an additional government-owned card.

Trust and surveillance

Yet, the real significance of the debate was to remind us of two facts, both of which explain the much greater resistance to government-sponsored identity cards than to smart cards run by business.

First, many government agencies are trusted much less than many businesses, to respect not merely the privacy rights of individuals, but a wide range of other rights. Whether there is or not a business case from government's point of view for combining the various applications from across departments and agencies on a multi-functional card, the public trusts government departments when sharing a card less than it would trust a cluster of businesses, not to use the opportunity for data matching and data mining, and not to use the resources generated for malign purposes. A report from the Data Protection Registrar in response to the Green Paper[80] outlined how current data protection principles – including rules over accuracy and appropriateness of information held – could prevent many of the abuses which might arise from an identity card scheme. The problem is that many citizens believe that government, which by tradition conducts many of its operations in secret, might well abuse these principles, especially if the temptation were to arise from the existence of a data-rich smart card.

Second, much of citizens' grudging acquiescence in the powers of the state is still based on the fact that the technological capacity and efficiency of the state in surveillance is limited. In short, it is in large part because the modern state still lacks the physical capacity for tyranny, that we are prepared to tolerate a situation in which it holds wide powers – even though we would not trust it with them if it were more efficient. As technological development increases that capacity, we may wish to set about its powers with new fetters. When, however, we cannot immediately think what new fetters would be workable, effective and fair, our first instinct remains that we would rather deny the state the physical capacity to exercise surveillance over us.

Of course, the public is not entirely consistent in this matter. Swayed by high-profile media coverage for street and city centre crime rates, it has been willing to accept the widespread introduction of closed circuit television and the gradual development of national criminal intelligence databases and services to the point where Britain now effectively has a national police force.

Identity cards, especially if they are smart, could certainly be the harbingers of wider state control and monitoring of individual citizens. Yet greater surveillance is not merely a matter of the powers of the police or government services to demand inspection of the cards when required. It would rather be the accompaniments for a national identity card scheme, which pose the greatest threat: a dedicated national database, shared by government departments, and possibly an individual identifying number. In combination, these two could enable departments to compose potent individual profiles and histories with much greater ease. Experience of identity cards in other countries has gone to show how harmful and intrusive the uses of an individual identifying number can be. Activities can be monitored over time, and data matched more comprehensively. Fraudulent use of 'borrowed' numbers has also been the bane of many national schemes. In Sweden recently, one innocent young mother received a care order for her son, with the justification that she was a registered drug abuser, accused of larceny, unpaid hospital bills and credit card debts. All this information was compiled through data networks and file mergers, and all originated from false use of her number.[81] In response to many such cases, the Swedish government is now planning to tighten use of identity numbers. In Britain there has been extensive media coverage of the intrusiveness in investigation and errors of identification of the Child Support Agency. Many people would be reluctant to trust such an agency with access to even more powerful technologies of surveillance.

Government-issued smart cards might not merely be multi-functional cards for a variety of public sector applications. They might become the standard platform on which private companies placed their applications by renting space on the chip. Because the architecture would be set by government, it is possible, perhaps even probable, that government would either specify the encryption systems to be used on the cards, or else would require the decryption keys to be escrowed with a government agency. If this were the case, there would be understandable fears that the issuing of a near universal government scheme was a quantum jump in government surveillance of citizens.

With potential abuses and threats like this all too apparent in many identity systems around the world, people tend to be highly suspicious of their introduction. Technologists may dismiss this reaction as Luddite. In fact, it probably represents something quite different – namely, a shrewd judgement about just which information capacities the state can be trusted with, subject to what safeguards.

The more interesting and important debate that we should be conducting now, concerns the safeguards that should be in place for the whole range of information technologies in governmental and commercial hands. Our priority is to reassure the public that the power they confer will not readily be abused and that people, as citizens and consumers, will have some control and privacy.

Privacy, power and law

Principles of privacy
How, then, can we develop a set of policies that will safeguard the things that are valuable in the ideas of privacy and confidentiality, that underlie the public concerns discussed above?

Definition
'Privacy' is not a clear concept or one that yields simple policy prescriptions for managing electronic database systems.[82] One prominent writer has defined it as 'the claim of individuals, groups or institutions to determine for themselves when, how, and to what extent information is communicated to others'.[83] The question is how this basic notion can practically be given force.

Clearly, in a law-governed society, such privacy claims sometimes have to be overridden. For all sorts of ordinary purposes, we need to allow people to learn about us without exercising specific control over every item of information they acquire. Where the police have evidence that leads them reasonably to suspect that a particular individual has committed a specific crime, their duties to investigate cannot be blocked by a right to privacy, although, of course, it does not follow that they can obtain information by any means whatsoever. Whenever someone enters into many forms of contract, these rights must be surrendered in greater or lesser degree. Insurance contracts, reasonably enough, commit us to provide insurers with sufficient access to information about ourselves to enable them to ensure that we are not simply exploiting the contract. A contract for a bank account is very difficult to manage without allowing the bank access to information about our financial situation, expenditures, etc.

Some commentators argue that the quantity of personal information on databases henceforth will mean that the idea of privacy gradually becomes obsolete.[84] But this need not be the case. A right can be meaningful and capable of practical expression, even if it is not absolute. Moreover, as various writers have argued, the claim of privacy is grounded in some rather fundamental human and organisational needs, such as solitude, intimacy, anonymity, barriers against unwanted intrusion, autonomy, self-evaluation, emotional release and limited and protected communication.[85]

Goals for public policy
In particular, the following two specific claims to rights can – as we shall argue in this chapter and the next – have practical application:
● the right to remain anonymous, at least in certain transactions where it is not necessary for the purpose of the transaction that the other party knows who one is;
● the right to control the uses others make of personal information they hold about one, that is, to consent to certain uses and to veto certain others.[86]

In this chapter, we first describe present British data protection laws and then assess their performance in securing these two rights. In the next chapter, we not only propose reforms to those laws, but go on to show that a wider strategy is also needed if they are to be given real meaning in the information age.

Data protection law

Data protection laws in most countries have usually concentrated their efforts upon sets of procedural principles about the terms on which personal data of certain sorts may be collected and handled, and enforcement efforts have focused on registration of databases.[87]

The principles

For example, the British 1984 Data Protection Act sets out eight general principles:[88]

1. The information to be contained in personal data shall be obtained, and personal data shall be processed fairly and lawfully.

2. Personal data shall be held only for one or more specified and lawful purposes.

3. Personal data held for any purpose shall not be used or disclosed in any manner incompatible with that purpose or those purposes.

4. Personal data held for any purpose shall be adequate, relevant and not excessive in relation to that purpose or those purposes.

5. Personal data shall be accurate and, where necessary, kept up to date.

6. Personal data held for any purpose or purposes shall not be kept for longer than is necessary for that purpose or those purposes.

7. An individual shall be entitled -

(a) at reasonable intervals and without undue delay or expense

(i) to be informed by any data user whether he or she holds personal data of which that individual is the subject; and

(ii) access to any such data held by a data user; and

(b) where appropriate, to have such data corrected or erased.

8. Appropriate security measures shall be taken against unauthorised access to, or alteration, disclosure or destruction of, personal data and against accidental loss

or destruction of personal data.

The exemptions

Certain data are exempt from the duty of registration and from the right of subject access granted by the seventh principle, namely that information which is:
● held only for domestic or recreational purposes;
● that the law requires to be made public;
● required to safeguard national security;
● held only for the purposes of running a payroll, accounts or pensions system;
● held by unincorporated members' clubs; or
● mailing lists of names, addresses and other information purely needed for distribution (this item may be removed in legislation to implement the October 1995 European Directive on data protection.)

Data are also be exempt from the right of subject access, where the data are:
● held for the purpose of preventing or detecting crime, apprehending offenders or assessing or collecting taxes;
● held for making judicial appointments;
● subject to legal professional privilege;
● statistics or research data only;
● 'back-up' data only;
● held by a credit reference agency (where other legislation provides for subject access); or where
● the content of the data would expose the user to criminal proceedings.

Specific limitations of the right of subject access apply in the case of health records, social work records, information protected by law, data held by financial regulatory bodies, and identifying data relating to individuals born as a result of fertilisation or embryology treatment.

The Act also creates certain criminal offences concerned with the disclosure of personal data to third parties not mentioned in the registry entry about the organisation's or individual's database, except where the disclosure is one:

- to which the data subject consents;
- to the data user's employees or agents;
- for the purpose of preventing or detecting crime, apprehending offenders or assessing or collecting taxes;
- made to safeguard national security;
- required by law, made for the purpose of obtaining legal advice, or in the course of legal proceedings; or
- done in an emergency to prevent injury or damage to anyone's health.

The 1995 European Directive

The October 1995 European Directive on data protection will require organisations to give data subjects greater control over the disclosure of their personal information, and provide advance notification of how consumers' names and the information attached to them is likely to be used.[89]

But the directive fails to specify in detail exactly how this should be implemented: it is for each member state to pass its own implementing legislation. The minimum required of a data user will probably be that anyone who wishes their name to be removed from a list should have that wish granted.

This is already common in the UK, through the use of telephone and mail preference services. In the absence of strong domestic political support for stronger measures, it is unlikely that this provision will require compulsory notification to consumers when information is passed to another agency. The British government is also reviewing the exemptions from subject access and from the disclosure rule, in the light of the European Directive.

However, when the Directive is implemented in British law, it will be first time that British statute law makes explicit mention of the concept of privacy, although it has recently been acknowledged in a judgement in the House of Lords that the 1984 Act is a partial privacy law.[90]

Evaluating data protection law today

British data protection law and the institutions that enforce it, as in many other countries, fail to reassure those concerned about abuse. Many of the principles have not adapted to the new technological applications, including interactive technologies able to store details about personal use and purchasing, and smart cards.[91] The 1980 OECD guidelines and the 1981 Council of Europe Convention established three themes for all legislation on personal information: any data system should be transparent to citizens, there should be well-defined limits to collection and use of data, and the data should be accurate and secure.[92] Together these principles are the foundation for any innovations or reform in data protection. A number of specific criticisms can be made of the design and operation of data protection in Britain.

Inadequate for modern technology
The law was drafted for another age. It neither protects against the new risks, nor encourages the use of the new opportunities created by modern technologies. It does not place any particular safeguards on the use of modern data matching and data mining techniques, beyond the general injunction not to use personal data for purposes other than those registered as the ones for which it was collected. If their purposes are sufficiently widely framed by careful drafting at the time of registration, then organisations are hardly constrained in their rights to match and mine. In this way, it is possible to conform to the letter of the law while violating its spirit.

Although the eighth principle has been supplemented by a more recent law creating new criminal offences concerned with 'hacking', there are still no specific duties on data users for example, to make all possible and appropriate use of 'pseudo-identifiers', or to make them ensure an audit trail is created that logs changes to or readings of each record, so that otherwise undetected accidental disclosures can be traced. The Data Protection Registrar advises many of these things, but has no power to impose specific security measures on any data user in advance, although the courts have powers to award compensation after the event for actual inaccuracy, loss or unauthorised disclosure that may result. Moreover, the Data Protection Registrar has no powers to award compensation, nor are experts aware of any court cases in which compensation has been awarded.

Limited rights for individuals

The law provides too few rights for data subjects and leaves most action in the hands of data users and regulators. The right to correction or erasure is limited. Opinions that do not claim to be statements of fact, however damaging, are neither accurate nor inaccurate and so not covered.

Action is largely in the hands of the data user, not the subject. It is for the data user to carry out or not carry out provision of subject access, disclosure, correction or erasure. The law provides no right for the subject physically to initiate these things from her or his own reader device or computer terminal. This leaves some problems in creating trust, because the data subject may not feel certain that any print-out or screen view of the data provided by the data user organisation is in fact a complete disclosure of all the data held.[93] It is not enough that individuals can apply to the Office of the Data Protection Registrar. If public distrust is running at high levels with vast numbers of databases containing personal information, no regulator could cope. Although the record of privacy commissioners in general is good, the risk of regulatory capture remains serious. Moreover, the costs of the time involved and the difficulty of invoking regulators inevitably means that many citizens will not resort to their services. If new technologies can enable us to find easier and more decentralised ways to enforce privacy, then we ought to use them.

The law provides rights that are in most cases after the event: there is no right to be alerted at the time that personal data of a particular sort have been created.[94]

Passive central regulation

In practice, the regulatory system is largely passive, because the authorities must wait for registration by data users and have no means of alerting themselves to the existence of data banks that ought to be registered.[95] The sheer proliferation of databases makes it almost impossible for any centralised system of regulation and enforcement to be effective. No privacy commission could ever have enough inspectors, enough information or respond sufficiently quickly, to all the possible risks of abuse, even if it were given draconian powers of inspection, seizure and penalty imposition. Rather, we need a new paradigm that places more control over the detection, correction and deletion of personal information in the hands of individuals.

Loopholes and enforceability

Some of the exemptions from the rights of subject access and the criminal offences of unauthorised disclosure are very widely drafted indeed. We saw in an earlier chapter that citizens are typically more distrustful of some government in these respects than they are of business. Both government agencies and private companies benefit from the exemptions from the rights of subject access in the case of national security, the prevention and detection of crime, and the assessment of taxes and duties. Although exemptions are to be scrutinised on a case-by-case basis, the broad drafting of the law makes it very difficult to challenge a refusal of subject access.

Because registered purposes can be drawn very widely, it can be very difficult for someone to enforce the fourth principle, that the information is irrelevant, inadequate or excessive for the purposes.

For all these reasons, data protection must be reformed and must be set in a wider framework of policies, if the public are to have solid reason to trust that smart technologies will not merely respect but could actually reinforce their privacy.

Smart card privacy: policy solutions

In this chapter, we bring together a number of policy recommendations that would, we believe, move the information society a long way towards a climate in which citizens and consumers could trust the organisations that issue them with smart technology products.

It is clear that there are several dimensions of the problem of securing appropriate rights to anonymity and rights to control use of personal data, and action is needed on each. We deal first with ways to ensure anonymity, looking first and briefly at the general regulation of strong cryptography, then at how policies could be put in place to stimulate the use of privacy-enhancing technologies. In the second half of the chapter, we deal with policies to increase personal control, beginning with the narrow issues of data protection, and then market structure issues in smart technology services, and finally to questions of data and card ownership. The chapter sets out a five-pronged strategy for buttressing reasonable anonymity and control, encompassing measures to stimulate the use of the right technologies, to reform regulation, to get private markets to provide the right services and to secure an ownership régime that maximises choice and control.

Regulating strong cryptography

The limits of coercion

The capacity of governments to restrict individuals' and companies' access to strong public key cryptography, and to compel them to use some form of escrow system, is now very limited. Now that many systems are widely and in some cases almost freely available, prohibition would be ineffective – a simple case of closing the stable door after the horse has bolted. Strong cryptography will be used in some privately issued smart card systems. In some cases, it will be an appropriate measure by which to respect privacy. In other cases, weaker systems or régimes of either private or government key escrow will be sufficient or more appropriate.

It is far beyond the purpose of this book to examine what this will mean for law enforcement agencies, or to suggest ways of overhauling their powers and strategies. There must, in any law-governed society, always be extraordinary situations, for which the police and security services can be given specific authority to override individuals and companies' rights of privacy that should otherwise be inviolate.

Goals

For the present purpose, the goal of public policy can be framed simply. It is to ensure sufficient cryptographic security of personal data accessed through smart cards to enable reasonable people to trust that their personal details will be confidential. If privacy must be overridden, access should be limited, specifically authorised for good legal reasons, and general 'fishing expeditions' either by governmental or private bodies should be prohibited.

A voluntary private escrow framework

It seems sensible to explore ways of introducing in Britain a light-touch regulatory scheme for private key escrow registries. Companies and individuals should not be compelled by law to use them. Rather, the market forces that make people want to seek out trustworthy partners to do business with should be harnessed to enable such private registries to develop their markets. A specific court order or warrant should be required before a registry may divulge a key to law enforcers.

Those who choose to use strong cryptography without depositing their private decryption keys with such bodies may have good and perfectly legal reason to do so. For example, banks issuing electronic cash may find that their consumers demand the security of knowing that no one can tamper with money held on their smart cards. However, once a working market system of private key escrow registries has developed, there might be a case for requiring a company or a government department to declare to the public whether or not it has escrowed its private decryption key with such a registry, so that citizens and consumers can come to their own conclusions about the privacy and security risks they face.

Privacy-enhancing technologies (PETs)

At present, our systems of law have done little to promote the use of technologies that respect anonymity, and there is a strong case for the next phase of regulation to experiment in this area.

Electronic privacy

As we have seen, cryptographic features can be provided in and on smart cards and the related central database systems and reader devices, which would go some way towards protecting the cardholder against intrusions into his or her personal privacy. Public policy should promote their use.

Some codes of practice are being developed by data users that encourage the use of such systems. In Britain, however, they are not commonly used.[96] However, the 1995 European Directive encourages the development of such codes and this could be a vehicle for promoting the use of technologies that will buttress privacy.

Information storage on its own is harmless. Only when this information is linked to an identifiable individual is it possible to compile matched sets of data, and invade the cardholder's privacy. One straightforward solution to dilemmas over privacy therefore is to reduce to the barest minimum the amount of identifying data.[97] The right to anonymity can be guaranteed electronically wherever it can be guaranteed in manual transactions. Thus, a purchase made using Mondex is anonymous to the seller in most situations, just as a cash purchase is.

Certain technologies can achieve this through use of an 'identity protector', which safeguards personal privacy against surveillance and monitoring by minimising the collection of identifiable data. In a smart card system, this protector could work by controlling the release of the cardholder's true identity to particular circumstances when this is absolutely required. A protector using advanced encryption techniques would generate pseudonymous identities as needed, and convert these into actual identities when and as desired – helping to reduce the sphere of identifiable data to manageable proportions.

How would these work? Encryption techniques are one means by which identity can be effectively protected. David Chaum of Digicash has devised a cryptographic technique for use with digital cash.[98] The recipient of the 'cash' via a smart card can be assured that the money is authentic and validated by the bank, but a 'blind signature' means that the retailer, for instance, would have no idea who sent it, and the bank would be unable to find out who has the money.[99] All that would be certain is the validity of the transaction – in exactly the same way as paying by cash. This technology has recently been tested in a European pilot scheme.

Pseudonymous identifiers also preserve anonymity by creating an identity for use by the system, yet one unconnected to the actual true identity of the individual. These have already been exploited in smart ticketing systems in public transport in Hong Kong and Singapore, and could easily be used in any scheme in which cards store value. Lastly, a trusted third party – such as a private key escrow registry – could keep a master key, linking the digital pseudonym with the real identity of the cardholder; this third party could be called upon under certain conditions, when it is essential to acquire the user's identity. When pseudo-identifiers or other privacy-enhancing technologies are used, health care records can be anonymous as far as the hospital's auditors or accountants are concerned.[100]

In short, there are a several ways by means of which the flow of identifiable data can be capped. Devising smart card systems to incorporate protection of privacy is not difficult. The public policy question is whether commercial and public issuers of smart cards systems can be persuaded to use these privacy-enhancing technologies. In many cases, there is no real business need for information identifying the individual cardholder to be held in places where every authorised reader device and every person using one can access it. Even multiple application cards could house a number of pseudo-identities on each application without great harm to commercial operations. Ultimately, the choice of these technologies will depend on the significance accorded by card issuers to maximum protection from fraud and compilation of information about particular identities. It may be that the business case for these latter features is insuperable. But it is also quite possible that with the rise of multiple forms of surveillance, of which smart cards are just one species, the demand for privacy will grow. In that case, successful applications will take account of popular demand and incorporate privacy-enhancing technologies in their designs. The choice between intrusive and privacy-enhancing technological forms is a crucial one; it is merely unfortunate that at present, the consumer is forced to accept his or her small card-carrying role in systems over which he or she has no control.

Strategies for government

Governments should play a leading role in promoting such technologies. In principle, they can (in order of least to greatest intervention):

● encourage standard setting bodies to adopt and promote standards for privacy-enhancing technologies;

● use their purchasing power to sponsor experiments, just as the European Commission has sponsored David Chaum's e-cash approach;

● use their purchasing power to franchise such approaches in public sector applications, either by direct government provision, simple purchase of service or through the Private Finance Initiative;

● use their fiscal authority to grant incentives through the tax system to users of PETs over users of more intrusive ones;

● take long-stop powers to regulate in the event that data users fail to regulate themselves to ensure the use of PETs, just as it has done with financial services and has threatened to do with newspapers;

● take powers of negative regulation allowing regulators, such as the Data Protection Registrar, to intervene to require the use of PETs in particular cases where intrusiveness seems particularly egregious, or in cases of actual abuse; or

● take powers of positive regulation to require the whole information industry to adopt such practices.

At this stage, governments have mainly used the first three less interventionist approaches. At this stage in the development of PETs, this is probably sound. There is, after all, little point in rushing to legislate before the technologies and their scope and capacities are well understood among data users, and before the willingness of business to use them without heavy pressure is known. However, there is an argument that over the next decade, as the technologies develop and cards proliferate, governments should signal unambiguously their willingness to use more interventionist tools if the industry fails to converge upon PETs as 'best practice'.

Principles of a data protection régime for the smart technology age

If citizens are to place their trust both in the smart technologies and in the businesses and public sector bodies that issue them, then we need a new régime of data protection that embodies a tougher set of principles than the present eight. We propose the following ten additions to the present law (some would require amendment of both British domestic law and the European Directives):

1. Except in the core coercive functions of government such as policing, data users should be required to obtain data subjects' permission individually on the uses to which the data are put.[101] If data subjects do not respond, they should be deemed not to have consented to any use of data held about them, and their record deleted. (The 1995 European Directive makes some tentative steps in this direction in Article 7, but does not enshrine in law the general principle that explicit consent of data subjects must be secured in advance for each specific use.)

2. The rules on disclosures to third parties should be tighter. Data users should be required either to show that they have received consent, or else to obtain specific and explicit permission in advance from the Data Protection Registrar where the data subject is unable to give or withhold consent and where the data user can make a powerful case for disclosure.

3. Data subjects should not only have the right of access, but they should be able to exercise it by means which are, organisationally and physically, independent of the data user. This could include using their own computer equipment, provided it uses reliable viewing or printing software.

4. Data subjects should have a right to be alerted – electronically and in 'real time' – about the creation of new categories of information of which they are the subject, and about major additions to the database record

about them. This might be achieved by the use of software that instructed reader devices to sound an alarm or to announce the making of the change on a machine's visual display. The data subject would then have the opportunity to make use of other data access services if he or she wished.

5. Data users should have to give much clearer and more specific purposes for the collection and maintenance of their data than they presently do. It may be worth exploring whether a 'multiple choice' list of highly specific purposes could be developed from which data users would have to choose.

6. The fourth principle should be extended to include a right to erasure of irrelevant or excessive material.

7. Data matching, especially in the public sector, should be subject to specific restrictions, such as time limits during which it must be completed or abandoned. Data obtained from data matching should not be added to databases unless it can be shown that these data are strictly necessary for the purpose for which the database was established. Wherever data matching yields data that are believed to be necessary, the addition should be subject to specific consent by the data subject.

8. Specific duties of security should be placed on data users, including those in the public sector, to use pseudo-identifiers, except where personal identification can be shown to be absolutely essential to the lawful purpose for which the data were collected. Secure audit trails should be maintained to track all reading and writing to records.

9. Exemptions from registration such as those concerned with national security, taxation and accounting should be much more tightly defined. National security exemptions should be granted only after a court order has been made, and registration has been shown to present a real and material risk. It should not be enough that a Cabinet Minister or government law officer simply signs a certificate saying that national security is at stake. Taxation, pensions and accounting databases should be registered unless there is very good reason otherwise.

Similarly, court orders should be required before denying subject access to their own records on databases kept for the prevention of crime and taxation.

10. The Office of the Data Protection Registrar should be given explicit duties and resources to take a more pro-active role in searching networks electronically for databases over which it should have jurisdiction, in inspecting premises and also in working with industry standards bodies and firms for the development of standards for privacy-promoting technologies.

Buttressing the rights of individuals to control much more of the information about them requires more than just strengthening data protection law. Laws that shield citizens from abuses of information do little to reduce the quantity of information stored by organisations. This is true, not least because data protection laws restricting the quantity of information collected to that is which 'adequate' and 'not excessive' for the purpose for which it was collected, are so vague as to be almost unenforceable, at least as long as we rely on the present system of detection and enforcement.

No central regulator can survey the whole field of the information society and comprehensively police privacy in it. In particular, some additional machinery is required if independent access is to be secured, and if this is to become a powerful market-based means for disciplining data users into respecting personal data confidentiality. In the next section, therefore, we propose a mechanism for achieving this.

Regulating the market structure for trust: structural separation

We have argued that data subjects should not only have the right of access, but they should be able to exercise it by means which are, organisationally and physically, independent of the data user. This could include using their own computer equipment, provided it uses reliable viewing or printing software.

Data access services

As long as few people own or rent their own reader devices, or have access to reader technology through an employer, this will be difficult to enforce.

What is needed, therefore, is a market in independent services for viewing personal data of which one is the subject comprehensively and accurately, together, perhaps, with services that propose and, in some circumstances, make corrections and deletions to data held by users, whether those data are located in the chip in the card or on a remote database to which the smart card acts as a key. Let us call these business activities, 'data access services'.

These access services could be delivered in a variety of ways. Companies could lease or sell a reader device to data subjects. They could, alternatively, offer data reading facilities at bank automated teller machines under partnership deals with banks.

Data subjects would, of course, pay for these services, but this could be done in a number of ways. Fee per item of service would probably be the basic form of payment. Club membership fees might be one possibility. Clubs might come to arrangements with data user companies whereby a data subject would buy a subscription to a data access company of their choice when they entered into a contract with the data user.

Distrust and demand for data access services

There will only be a business case for data access companies if the public disquiet about data protection in the smart technology age – as reported in surveys such as the Henley Centre Dataculture research – actually turns into demand for independent viewing. In principle, there is no reason why it should not. An entrepreneurial data access company would make it part of its marketing mission to stir up demand on the basis of such widespread public attitudes.

Firewalls

There are two arguments that data user companies and data access companies should not be vertically integrated. The first is that consumers do not trust integrated companies because there may be a conflict of interest from the point of view of the consumer. Secondly, data access services may be required to use the data user's own software and outlets. This is analogous to an exclusive distribution agreement, that prevents the consumer from shopping around for the 'downstream' data access services.

How might structural independence of data users and data access service-issuers be achieved in the smart technology age?

One strategy is to secure the independence of firms that provide access services from firms and public sector agencies that have any interest in writing to or reading from cards, by introducing new stock market rules on ownership.

Essentially, data users – as defined by the 1984 Data Protection Act – or any other person or organisation that has an interest in securing that electronic data be written or read, could not collectively or individually own more than, say, a 10 per cent stake in a data access services company. There would be, in effect, a structural separation in the market between companies that provide smart cards and companies that provide cardholders, or data subjects, with a comprehensive view of the data either held in their cards or to which the card grants access.

This would inhibit some, but not all, institutional investors from owning equity in data access companies. They might be permitted, however, to hold certain types of bonds or non-voting stock subject to a rule that prevented institutional investors from placing conditions on the companies that interfered with the data access services. This would enable data access companies to raise capital, other than through debt, without undermining their independence.

Obviously, data access services companies would need to have some relations with data user companies. For example, they would have to have the right to buy, lease or franchise the means of getting to the data. This might include being granted special authorisations such as passwords, decryption keys, and validation of on-line transactions.

To ensure that these contracts with card issuers did not compromise the independence of viewing, there would have to be legal restrictions to prevent clauses being inserted that fettered the data access services companies in their ability to offer independent views of personal data.

Limited demand and contestability

If demand for data access services proved to be limited, the markets might come to believe that the existence of the law providing for structural separation effectively commits the government to the continued existence of at least one independent data access company. This might make the price of shares in the remaining one company or few companies artificially inflated.

Government should signal unequivocally that it would not bail out such companies. It is for individual consumers, not government, to decide whether their fears about privacy should lead them to demand data access services to set their minds at rest about what data are held about them.

Suppose, then, that no data access companies proved viable. Would the policy then have failed and should the structural separation law then be repealed? No. The very existence of the law may itself be a force that disciplines data users. Much as monopolists may be kept on their toes not by actual competition but the knowledge that their market is contestable, so data user companies issuing cards may take adequate care of privacy and data confidentiality precisely for fear that if they do not, card-issuing companies could exploit their errors.

Learning from experience about how to implement separation

The analogies

There are precedents from which we can draw for such a course of policy and to which we need to look in order to understand how implementation problems can be overcome. Britain and other countries have had experience of such stock market 'firewalls' legislation over many years, in at least three distinct ways.

First, under the title of 'cross-media' ownership rules, legislation restricts the extent to which newspaper and broadcasting firms can achieve market domination. In that case, the purpose of structural independence is not directly to ensure that consumers trust in the content of the output, but rather diversity and pluralism in the marketplace of ideas.

Second, several countries use financial services ownership rules requiring market separation. In the United States, for example, the Glass-Steagall Act regulates banking to restrict the kinds of companies in which banks may take equity stakes and the kinds of contracts, partnerships and other arrangements into which they may enter.

Third, anti-trust or competition law provides a general long-stop mechanism whereby structural separations can be required between firms that would otherwise either integrate services against the interests of the consumer – which is the case for structural separation of data access and data user companies – or else to prevent market domination where that works against the consumer or the public interest. Implementation is the responsibility of executive agencies (in Britain, the Office of Fair Trading or the Monopolies and Mergers Commission; in the European Union, the Directorate-General IV of the Commission), and, in the final instance the courts (in the USA, the courts are the enforcers of first instance).

Obviously, none of these three types of regulation are entirely problem-free, and large literatures have grown up criticising various solutions adopted around the world for media pluralism, and for preventing monopoly and restrictive practices. Nevertheless, they enable us to identify some key lessons about how unbundling the vertical integration of data user and data access services would have to be implemented and enforced.

Market definitions
It is clear from the anti-trust experience that the markets into which integration is to be prevented must be very tightly defined. The fact that companies will have an incentive to find loopholes or ways around the firewalls suggests not only that ownership restrictions need to be soundly based, but that formulations are found in law that will prevent other kinds of arrangements between the two kinds of companies from undermining the purpose of the separation. Thus, software leasing contracts for password and decryption systems would have to be monitored carefully by the enforcement agencies. A particular difficulty is that some of the prime suspects, in the public mind, are government departments. Experience in benefits, immigration and other fields suggests that enforcing structural separation against government requires a system in which judicial review would only be open once the tribunal route had been exhausted.

Firewalls and transactions
There is a serious question about whether what, if any, minority stake is acceptable and if so, on what terms. We have suggested a 10 per cent threshold, but there may be a case for a slightly lower or higher one. Beyond the separation of equity stakes, it will be important to prevent data-using companies from using loans and more complex financial instruments to undermine separation by imposing conditions that would compromise the integrity of the services offered. These companies would therefore be able to raise debt finance from banks and other financial institutions, but lenders would be debarred from placing conditions on that debt that, for

example, disabled the company from offering data access services to that bank's personal datasets.

A data access company that is denied by a data user – say, a bank, or a health insurance company – an agreement to rent its decryption software for the purpose of offering data access services to that bank's or insurer's consumers might feel aggrieved. If a simple denial were involved, then it might be reasonable for the law to intervene, on the grounds that some form of exclusive distribution appears to be in use. However, if the problem was simply that the price offered by the data access company was too low, then it would be unreasonable interference with freedom of contract for the law to compel the data user to offer the contract at a price the data access company would want. The only exception should be where the data access company could convince the enforcement agency that the price demanded by the data user was far beyond the market value of the contract. This would not be straightforward, but it presumably demands no more of the courts or regulators than is already demanded in considering other kinds of exclusive distribution agreements.

Enforcement
Separation requires a system of enforcement. Leaving matters to the courts has, on the face of it, certain merits. In particular, it allows individuals and companies to bring actions in their own names. However, since individuals would – in the present fiscal climate – almost certainly not be eligible for Legal Aid, the real value of this advantage might be limited. An executive agency might make determinations quicker, and be more willing to look at the spirit rather than the letter of suspect arrangements. However, if experience of the Monopolies and Mergers Commission and Directorate-General IV of the European Commission is anything to go by, they tend to be readily captured by monopoly business interests or political commitments to certain firms. Self-regulatory systems such as those in use for financial services firms

may be insufficient to meet public concerns about the need for independence.

However, there may be a case for considering a specialist tribunal to which individuals could bring their own cases, but where costs would not be awarded; the enforcement of its orders would be a matter, ultimately, for the civil courts. Some limited extra-territorial jurisdiction would be needed for the tribunal and the courts, because many of the firms involved in these industries are transnational.

Penalties for violation of the structural separation rules should be graduated. Clearly, the tribunal should have power to order divestment of one or other side of the business. Should the tribunal have the power to award compensation? Unless it has that power, it is not clear that many individuals who feel aggrieved that they have been denied independent data access services will in fact make the effort to bring cases. On the other hand, any damages would have to be awarded for actual harm to an individual caused by violations of data protection law, not by unlawful vertical integration.

Data access services companies which have been denied by data users software agreements enabling them to offer consumers access to data on, for example, bank, retail or health insurance smart cards, might feel aggrieved and might be motivated to seek compensation for lost revenues. However, this would be limited to the cases where refusal to contract on the part of the data user was deemed unlawful (see point 1 above).

The tribunal should only have the role of enforcing structural separation. Actual violations of data protection law would remain a matter for the Data Protection Registrar. While the two regulators would have to work together, their core competencies would be quite distinct and a merger would be unlikely to be effective.

Citizen ownership: personal data and cards
Greater individual control over the use of personal data is our central policy aim. Therefore, it makes sense to

consider what role there could be for greater personal ownership in this field.

At present, the companies and government departments that issue cards and hold personal data own both the cards and the data. This has a three major implications.

Any corrections or deletions are, at least in the first instance, a matter for these data users, and only the Data Protection Registrar or the courts can require them to make corrections and deletions. Where card-carrying consumers want viewing access to personal data about them, or want to insist that certain commercial uses are not made of those data, it takes the special provisions of the Data Protection Act to grant them the right to override the wishes of the owners of the data. At present, cardholders are generally excluded from determining who should have access to the card, and what levels of personal information are available to which organisations.[102]

Finally, the fact that data users own the cards and the applications means that if they want to make sure that their card contains only the applications they themselves consent to being put there, then they can insist upon this. Consumers cannot at present decide, if their wallets are overly full with cards, that they would like to combine applications onto one or fewer cards just as they might do with files on their own floppy disks. Could it be otherwise?

Personal data ownership

Someone who takes seriously the idea of 'informational self-ownership', espoused by the German courts in data protection cases, might want to suggest that individuals could be given intellectual property rights in personal data about themselves.

Full ownership of personal data about oneself is almost certainly impossible. Certain data are created by government with a duty to disclose them in certain circumstances. If we all 'owned' the data about endorsements on our driving licences, then presumably we could decide whether or not it should appear in our smart card driving licence or be displayed to traffic police and the courts, which would defeat the purpose of the endorsement system. Even in the case of private sector cards, full ownership cannot include the right to change, hide or falsify all sorts of personal data. For example, if we owned the data stored on our electronic purses about how much money we have, we could all print money, defraud the financial system and create inflationary havoc.

Nor, of course, do companies and government agencies 'own' personal data in the sense that they may destroy, hide or falsify it as they wish. If they do so, they risk being brought to book for fraud or breach of contract or, in the case of a government agency, by way of judicial review for violation of the *Wednesbury* principles that govern how, in general, public agencies must conduct their business.

Clearly, then, ownership rights in personal data must always be attenuated in some way. Defining a workable and fair set of qualifications upon individual ownership of personal data is not straightforward. For example, should certain sorts of information be subject to a duty to disclose in particular circumstances? Civil libertarians have long argued that citizens in a liberal society should have the right, not merely not to incriminate themselves by refusing to divulge certain facts, but to remain anonymous, if they wish to do so. Probably, any duties of disclosure to the police that went beyond those presently in place for personal information would probably be politically unacceptable.

Yet even defining the content of our information disclosure duties in pre-electronic practices is not always easy. In the insurance context, there will always be dispute between insurers and individuals about what information is relevant to determining a premium. The exact information disclosure duties implicit in an insurance contract are always unclear. Companies can insert into policy documents duties on policy-holders to declare specific sorts of information from which the insurer can draw inferences (e.g. from marital status to risk of contracting a sexually transmitted disease, or from postcode to risk of burglary), but policy-holders may reasonably object to the inferences drawn. Moreover, insurance policies could never contain a complete list of all the factors that might be relevant in any individual case. Therefore a legal duty that qualified personal data ownership, placing a duty on individuals to disclose all 'relevant' personal data to insurers, electronically or manually, would be of no help in resolving such disputes either.

There is, therefore, probably little to be gained by trying to re-write the rules on ownership of personal data.

Card ownership

Ownership of cards and applications, however, is a different matter entirely. Is there any reason why individuals should not own the cards with which they are issued, and decide for themselves which applications to combine on any single card?

Companies and government departments usually want ownership of the cards they issue for several reasons.

First, there is the issue of physical branding. There are alternative ways of ensuring that physical branding is retained, even if individuals could move applications between cards as they pleased to create their own multi-functional cards. Logos could be made smaller and contracts with consumers could include a consumer's duty to keep the logo on the card currently holding the corresponding application. In time, perhaps, the need for physical branding might be replaced by a culture in which electronic branding mattered much more.

Second, data users do not necessarily trust each other to write applications that will respect the electronic firewalls, often built into the chip operating system, which protect their own application from interference by others. This may be a concern in the case of electronic purses, where a bank might fear fraudulent siphoning off of money in fictitious purchases on the card. In the cases of so-called 'loyalty' cards for other companies, the audit trail of consumer behaviour and purchases is information that might be commercially valuable to a competitor. There are, however, a number of solutions to this problem that are compatible with consumers making their own decisions about the location of applications on smart cards. Technology may help, as chip architectures provide greater security. Specific contracts between groups of companies, warranties or collective self-regulation institutions could all have a role to play here.

Third, there is concern that consumers will not be prepared to pay more in bank charges, insurance premiums, driving licence fees, etc. for the qualified ownership rights over cards that are necessary to allow them to make up their own multi-functional cards. Card issuers will argue that there are real costs that will have to be passed on to consumers of allowing 'do-it-yourself' multi-functionality: these include the costs of the security architecture, the costs of reaching, drafting and enforcing the agreements with other card application issuers and with the consumers. However, as the unit cost of smart technologies falls and as the gains in convenience and time for consumers grow, this may not be such a great problem.

Policies to stimulate consumer ownership
In our view, then, there is a strong case for requiring companies and government departments to offer at least some cards that would be owned by consumers, in order that they should have the right to move applications at will between cards and destroy or not use those cards in which they choose not to leave applications.

Will competitive pressures lead data users to offer cards on these terms, or is there any case for intervention?

It is certainly possible that at least some companies will be willing to offer consumer-owned cards. However, others will be more reluctant. Unless almost all major card issuers are willing to offer consumer-controlled versions of their cards and applications, the right will not mean very much because it will not ensure extensive multi-functionality. Therefore, there may be a case for government intervention to require consumer-owned versions of cards and applications to be available. Presumably, at least initially, there would be a price difference between cards owned by the issuer and cards owned by the cardholder.

If companies chose to demand extortionate rates for consumer-owned cards, and if the ordinary competitive pressures did not lead at least some firms to defect from such an implicit cartel by offering cheaper rates, then the duty to offer consumer-owned versions would have been subverted. In that case, there would be a case for further government intervention. That should take the form, not of price regulation, but of action by the competition authorities such as the Director-General of Fair Trading. Naturally, companies and government departments would remain free, additionally, to offer cards that they own to those consumers who are not willing to pay a reasonable increment in price for the freedoms offered by ownership.

Conclusion

Trust, control and the multi-functional smart card
Smart technologies offer enormous benefits, in principle,
to citizens and consumers, government and business.
However, citizens and consumers must be persuaded to
trust in the new smart technologies, if the information
society is to be both a reality and a boon. We have argued
that people will trust in these technologies when they
can choose anonymity where they want it and have
greater control over the use of the personal information
held about them.

Our strategy has five main elements: first we need to
re-think our approach to the regulation of strong
cryptography. Prohibition is neither feasible nor
desirable, but there is a role for a voluntary system of
private key escrow.

Second, government must promote the use of privacy-
enhancing technologies.

Third, data protection laws should be strengthened. Of
our proposed reforms to data protection, the most radical
is the reversal of the current right of initiative, placing a
duty on data users to gain express consent from data
subjects for the use to which they want to put the data.

Fourth, we need a system of structural separation to

ensure that independent access to data can be guaranteed if consumers and citizens need it, and ownership rights over cards to enable citizens to make their own choices about the risks they want to take. Structural separation for data access services provides a discipline on data users. If public trust in their respect for privacy declines, then demand for independent data access services would rise. That would indicate to data users that they were facing consumer resistance and they would risk losing some of their business.

Fifth, a market in consumer-owned cards should be created, if necessary by government intervention. This would be a secondary market in trustworthiness. Individuals should have the right to choose a card that they own. If privacy is their main concern, they will choose an issuer that markets the privacy-enhancing technologies built into their cards. Civil libertarians, for example, should be able to buy 'blank' cards with built-in PETs and secure architecture, from the Electronic Frontier Foundation or Privacy International, if those organisations are willing to offer them, and then decide which combinations they will risk putting on different directories in the same card.

This vision is quite the reverse of the model suggested by the Home Secretary, the Rt. Hon. Michael Howard MP, in his consultation paper on identity cards. That paper hinted seriously that one option would be a government issuer-controlled multi-functional card, in which citizens would have little or no choice about which applications co-reside and perhaps no choice about the privacy system, if any, that would govern them. We have seen that public trust in the willingness of many government agencies to respect privacy is lower even than that placed in many areas of businesses. Experience suggests that distrust is not entirely unreasonable.

Where the 'Howard card' is an essentially authoritarian instrument, our proposal is for a more market-based instrument, in which the role of government is to align the incentives within the market to ensure privacy, trust and individual access and control.

The debate in the next decade need not be a continued sterile confrontation between civil libertarians and the interests of business and government. It could be a fruitful collaboration between technology, the assurance of privacy and the power of the market with light-touch regulation. Our argument is that the policy framework should be put in place as soon as possible.

Glossary

Application: A category of activity or transaction for which a specific procedure in software and data handling is written. Examples include electronic cash, store 'loyalty' monitoring and points systems, payphone points purchasing systems, health records management systems, social security claim system for an individual claimant. The software for an application may be wholly or partly stored in the chip in a smart card, or the chip may contain only data that are activated by an application stored in a reader device or a remote central computer accessed through a reader device.

Architecture: The underlying structure of hardware and software in a smart card system that supports applications in the card.

Audit trail: An electronic record, stored either in a chip in a smart card or else on a remote computer, of a transaction that the chip has made with authorised reader devices.

Biometric identifier: Any uniquely identifiable part of the human anatomy or physical characteristics of an individual, that can be used for the purposes of indentification. These can include a retinal scan, thumb scan, fingerprint, hand geometry, DNA reading or lip print, or a simple full-face photograph that has been digitised.

Cardholder: The individual carrying a smart card, to whom personal information stored in or accessible through the card relates, and who is legally entitled to conduct transactions using it.

Card-issuer: An organisation owning an information and business system in which smart cards are used, and which provides individuals (cardholders) with such cards.

Closed circuit television (CCTV): A video camera system connected in real time to a monitor or video recorder, usually used as a device for physical surveillance of all individuals moving within the range of vision of the camera.

Co-residence: The storage of multiple applications in the chip in a single smart card, usually in different directories.

Contactless card: A type of smart card which can be used in a transaction without having to be inserted physically into a drive in a reader device, but which can conduct the transaction at some distance from the reader device. The chip in the card receives power from the read-and-write device, allowing the card and reader/writer to transfer signals and information by radio, laser or other means.

Data access services: The services, provided to data subjects, of providing accurate and comprehensive views of personal data concerning them held on a database, making proposals for – or, if authorised, actually carrying out – corrections and deletions.

Data matching: The process of comparing and analysing

records about a data subject from two or more sources.

Data mining: Undertaking data profiling and data matching in as comprehensive a fashion as possible to build up a very detailed picture of what is known about a data subject.

Data profiling: The process of automatically processing computerised information to identify target data subjects (e.g. potential customers) on the basis of their characteristics.

Data protection: 1. The legal imposition of control, or limit, on the collection, use and disclosure of personal information.
2. The executive activity of carrying out and implementing this form of regulation.

Data user: an organisation, agency or company that collects personal data, uses and manipulates them, and controls their content.

Data subject: An individual described by any set of personal data or to whom those data relate.

Decryption: The process of converting encrypted information into readable matter.

Directory: A distinct area of memory (or other data storage device) in the chip in a smart card, within each of which an application may reside.

E-cash^{TM}: Trademark for the variety of electronic cash offered by the Netherlands-based company, Digicash, headed by David Chaum.

Electronic cash: Currency, accepted as legal tender within an electronic payment system, usually taking the form of electronic credits, dispensed when an instruction is issued by the application to a 'till' to withdraw currency from its memory during a transaction.

Electronic purse: A smart card system that dispenses electronic cash in small amounts, for use during transactions. The sums are small enough so that usually no Personal Identity Number is considered necessary.

Electronic token: A pre-paid entitlement to a specified quantity of a certain service, such as transport, pay telephones, film admissions or car parking, usually measured in units of electronic cash or other credit or points system, that may be stored in a smart card.

Electronic tolling: A means of automatically charging vehicles for the use of roads. Tolling can use smart card systems, where the card is embedded in the vehicle. Units are deducted as the card passes underneath gantries at various points along the road.

Encryption: The process of converting information into a string of symbols that means nothing to a person for whom it is not intended. This is done by the use of an algorithm or key to encode the information, and another key to decrypt it.

Escrow: "Private decryption key escrow", to give the full title, is a system for the management of strong cryptography. Government no longer prohibits individuals and companies from using these methods, but provides enabling legislation for approved private bodies to act as registries, holding decryption keys on a confidential basis for those individuals and companies. A key might be split between several agencies. Government law enforcement agencies could only insist that a registry divulge keys that have been "escrowed" to them, if they can obtain a warrant from a court on the basis either of a vital and immeiate threat to national security or that the key is necessary in order to obtain crucial evidence in the investigation of a specific crime to which the individual or company is linked by evidence already in their possession. Such a system has a number of advantages for companies and individuals over absolute privacy for encryption. The registries can market themselves by stressing the quality of their research into the trustworthiness of their clients, and so the fact that a key is placed with a reputable registry can act as a "digital reputation" of some value when trading electronically. Companies can also access the ergistry's copy of their key is their own copy os lost, corrupted or damaged. An example of a law establishing the system is Utah state's Digital Signatures Act 1995. "Compulsory escrow", which is not advocated in this book, is a system whereby government legally compels all individuals and companies to escrow their keys with a government agency, for example, by requiring them to use a chip that can only use an encryption system to which government holds decryption keys: an example of this is the US federal government proposal for the "Clipper chip".

Firewalls: 1. Security procedures expressed in software that prevent ordinary use of an application during foreseeable kinds of transactions from having any consequences for any other application co-resident in a chip, for example, in another directory and especially for any data handled by the second application.
2. Legal restrictions on the ownership of certain types of companies by other types of companies, usually introduced for the purpose of achieving structural separation of markets.

Identity card: A document, file, or application put into a paper card, magnetic stripe card or a smart card which contains identifying and other information relating to an individual, and which has the primary purpose of proving the individual's identity to an organisation.

Information society: A vision of society, the economy and

polity in which most ordinary commercial, governmental and personal relationships and transactions are transformed, wholly or partly, by the fact that they are conducted by means of information and communications technology, include information superhighways, smart cards, video conferencing, multimedia and electronic publishing, virtual reality, artificial intelligence, robotics, electronic purchasing, etc.

Information superhighway: A metaphor for a system or network of electronic links connecting homes and businesses, along which large amounts of information can travel at high speed. Sometimes applied (stressing the word 'super') strictly to systems that use fibre-optic cabling with very large bandwidth. Less strictly used to describe networks that use traditional twisted pair copper wiring installed originally for voice telephony and now used by most personal computer modems for services such as those provided over the Internet.

Liquid crystal display: An electronic display mechanism based on the passage of electric currents through crystals, used for presenting information on a screen or any small digital display.

Loyalty scheme: A commercial scheme, often implemented using a smart card, which entitles regular ('loyal') users of a retail service to extra benefits such as price reductions or air miles. Information about the customer's purchasing habits can be stored either in a smart card, or in a central database. Loyalty schemes run by retailers need not make use of smart cards, but the new technology is proving increasingly popular.

Magnetic stripe: A set of magnetised tracks held on the back of cards which contain information, such as the primary account number (on a bank card) and the expiry date of the card. The main difference between a magnetic stripe card and a smart card is the site where the processing takes place. With a magnetic stripe card this happens in a central database, whereas on a smart card the chip in the card carries out some processing locally.

Microprocessor: The source of computing power in the chip in a smart card, which enables the card both to store information and to respond to signals and data transferred from outside the card.

Mondex™: An electronic purse scheme run by a partnership of Midland and National Westminster banks, which is currently being piloted in Swindon, and which the partnership expects to franchise to associates around the world.

Multi-functional cards: Smart cards containing a variety of separate applications, which are independent from each other, and accessible – in theory and ideally – only through application-specific reader devices.

Off-line: A transaction or exchange (of information, entertainment or money) isolated in space, with no connection to a wider network or communications system.

On-line: A transaction or exchange which takes places over a network such as the telephone network, making a distinct call over that network and involving electronic traffic between a computer (e.g. a smart card and reader device) and – usually – a remote central database computer.

Pay-per-view television: A system of television broadcasting in which the viewer pays for each programme watched.

Personal identification number (PIN): A number known only to the individual cardholder, used as a password to an application, which can help provide secure access to a service or facility.

Privacy-enhancing technology (PET): A technology or design of a technological system, useable in a smart card system, which minimises the amount of information connected to an identifiable individual.

Pseudo-identifier: An alternate digital identity for a data subject, distinct from the subject's actual identity, which can be used to identify the cardholder within a smart card system without revealing to the data user who that subject really is, but allowing data manipulation to take place.

Stored value card: A smart card which can carry and exchange units of value such as money or payphone credits.

Structural separation: A system of restrictions on ownership, loans, and other transactions that creates two distinct fields of activity or markets where otherwise services might be integrated vertically (e.g. from production to distribution, or from data using to data access) or concentrated horizontally (e.g. an industry that has been monopolised). See 'firewall'.

Super smart cards: A new generation of smart cards, currently in the late stages of development, containing a microprocessor, a keyboard, a liquid crystal display and their own power source, enabling the card to carry out some transactions or provide data access services without having to come into contact with a separate a card reader device.

Swipe card: A magnetic stripe card that can be used in a transaction by 'swiping' through a reader device, in order to transfer funds or to provide selective access to a building. By swiping the card through a reader device information can be relayed to a central database, which can check that the cardholder has sufficient funds or validate the card.

Upstream and downstream services: Upstream services are those which are provided first in a logical sequence setting out the processes involved from production to distribution and consumption. Downstream services are those provided later.

Notes

1. See e.g. Federal Trust for Education and Research, 1995, *Network Europe and the information society,* Federal Trust for Education and Research, London.

2. For an unambiguous statement of the creed of authoritarianism, see Scruton, R., 1980, *The meaning of conservatism,* Penguin, Harmondsworth: 16: '... no citizen [is] possessed of a natural right that transcends his obligation to be ruled.'

3. Wright, T., 1993, *Smart cards,* Information and Privacy Commissioner, Ontario: 4.

4. Wright, T., 1993, *Smart cards,* Information and Privacy Commissioner, Ontario: 11.

5. Central Computer and Telecommunications Agency (CCTA), 1994, *Smart cards: opportunities for public sector applications,* HMSO, London: 7.

6. Heath, W., 1995, *Wired Whitehall,* Kable, London; Swinden, K. and Heath, W., 1996, *Tomorrow's town hall,* Kable, London.

7. Chaum, D., 1992, 'Achieving electronic privacy', *Scientific American,* August, 96-101.

8. 'Cash versus cashless', *Financial Times,* 20.2.96.

9. Estimate in 'From gimmick to necessity', *Financial Times,* 12.1.94.

10. 'The world in your wallet', *Siemens Review,* June 1995, vol. 62:5.

11. Parliamentary Office of Science and Technology, 1994, 'Personal identification technologies', *POST note* 54, HMSO, London.

12. 'What a calling card!', *Siemens Review,* June 1995, vol. 62: 10.

13. Wright, T., 1993, *Smart cards*, Information and Privacy Commissioner, Ontario: 15.

14. Mandell, L., 1990, *The credit card industry: a history*, Twayne, Boston: 150-151.

15. 'Purse roll-out in Portugal', *Smart Card News*, July 1995, vol. 4, no. 7: 132.

16. 'The colour of money', *Wired* magazine, February, 96.

17. Associated Payment and Clearing Systems (APACS) is planning to install the infrastructure to use smart credit cards in Britain by 1997. French credit cards already carry both computer chips and magnetic stripes. Parliamentary Office of Science and Technology, 1994, 'Personal identification technologies', *POST note* 54, HMSO, London.

18. 'Mondex: security by design', *City security*, June 1995.

19. 'Tomorrow's banks are here', *Sunday Times*, 4.2.96.

20. 'Big three rift exposed by breakaway Europay', *Smart Card News,* July 1995.

21. 'Where money isn't everything', *Guardian*, 11.1.96.

22. The role of smart cards in an international system of health care is a prominent part of the current investigation by the G-7 and EU into the 'information society': Commission of the European Communities, 1995, 'G-7 information society conference pilot projects', paper given at the G-7 conference, 'Information society', Brussels, 25-26.2.95.

23. Dix, A., 1995, 'Identity cards in Germany', paper presented at the conference, *Identity cards: putting you in the picture*, 23.6.95, London.

24. Central Computer and Telecommunications Agency (CCTA), 1994, *Smart cards: opportunities for public sector applications*, HMSO, London: 6.

25. Central Computer and Telecommunications Agency (CCTA), 1995, *Smart cards case study: the Care Card*, Exmouth Healthcare Project, HMSO, London.

26. Privacy Commissioner for Australia, 1995, *Smart cards: implications for privacy*, Privacy Commissioner for Australia, Canberra: 24-26.

27. The proposed introduction of health cards in Australia, the US and New Zealand recently caused particularly intense controversies. Davies, S., 1996, *Big brother: Britain's web of surveillance and the new technological order*, Pan Books, London: 160. In the UK, there is now a debate about security, confidentiality and public trust in information systems for medical records: the British Medical Association has now published a report commissioned by its Medical

Information Technology Committee, setting out standards and principles: Anderson, R.J., 1996, *Security in clinical information systems*, British Medical Association, London.

28. Technology Development Centre, 1995, *Telematics Finland*, Technology Development Centre, Helsinki.

29. Central Computer and Telecommunications Agency (CCTA), 1995, *Smart cards case study: the OneCard*, Greater Manchester Passenger Transport Authority, HMSO, London.

30. Privacy Commissioner for Australia, 1995, *Smart cards: implications for privacy*, Privacy Commissioner for Australia, Canberra: 21.

31. 'The world in your wallet', *Siemens Review*, vol 62, June 1995: 5.

32. The Henley Centre for Forecasting, 1995, *Dataculture: privacy, participation and the need for transparency in the information age*, Henley Centre for Forecasting, London: 34.

33. Central Computer and Telecommunications Agency (CCTA), 1995, *Smart cards case study: the Quantum Card*, British Gas, HMSO, London.

34. The case for efficiency and citizen involvement in government through smart identity cards has recently been made by Stevens, J. and Worsfold, J., 1995, *On line in time: the case for a smart citizens' card for Britain*, John Stevens MEP, London.

35. 'Lilley's benefit smart card "is a dumb move"', *The Times*, 18.10.95.

36. Central Computer and Telecommunications Agency (CCTA), 1995, *Smart cards: opportunities for public sector applications*, HMSO, London: 4.

37. Privacy Commissioner of Australia, 1995, *Smart cards: implications for privacy*, Privacy Commssioner for Australia, Canberra: 11.

38. Wright, T., 1993, *Smart cards*, Information and Privacy Commissioner, Ontario: 23.

39. 'Cash versus cashless', *Financial Times* 20.2.96.

40. 'Cash versus cashless', *Financial Times* 20.2.96.

41. Birch, D., and McEvoy, N., 1996, *Smart cards and superhighways: the technology-driven denationalisation of money*, Centre for the Study of Financial Innovation, London; Birch, D., 1996, 'Downloadsamoney', *Demos Quarterly, 8*.

42. Wright, T., 1993, *Smart cards*, Information and Privacy Commissioner, Ontario: 19.

43. The only place which currently operates a system of smart cards along these lines is Northern Thailand: Davies, S., 1996, *Big brother: Britain's web of surveillance and the new technological* *order*, Pan, London: 167.

44. Stevens, J. and Worsfold, J., 1995, *On line in time: the case for a smart citizen's card for Britain*, John Stevens MEP, London.

45. Heath, W., 1995, 'Close encounters of the digital kind', *Missionary Government, Demos Quarterly 7*: 42-43.

46. A good basic introduction is Channel 4 Programme Support Online, 1995, *Cybersecrecy: code-breakers and code-makers*, Channel 4, London.

47. The best known is Philip Zimmermann's PGP ('Pretty good privacy') system, which is available with supporting materials very widely on the Internet.

48. The activities of a small group of 'crypto-anarchists' arguing that rights to absolute privacy should override the claims of government law enforcers effectively mirror, as hopes, the fears of some government agencies. A leading light in this movement is Tim May: see his 1995 paper, 'Crypto anarchy and virtual communities', available on http://thumper.vmeng.com/pub/rah/anarchy.html.

49. The Electronic Privacy Information Centre (EPIC), the Electronic Frontier Foundation, Privacy International, and the magazine *Wired* have provided much of the co-ordination for this campaign. All have extensive materials on these issues available from their World Wide Web sites.

50. The leading advocate in the USA of key escrow is Professor Dorothy Denning of Georgetown University. See her 1996, 'The future of cryptography', available on http://cosc.georgetown.edu/~denning/crypto/Future.html.

51. The full text of the legislation is available on http://evolvingtech.com/007/SB008 2.html.

52. Denning, D., 1996, 'The future of cryptography', available on World Wide Web site: http://www.cosc.georgetown.edu/~denning/crypto/Future.html: 5.

53. Koops, B-J., 1996, 'Crypto law survey', available on http://cwis.kub.nl/~frw/people/koops/lawsurvy.htm.

54. Labour Party, 1995, *Communicating Britain's future*, Labour Party, London: 14.

55. 'Consumers' views on technology and finance', ICL/MORI survey, 11. 95.

56. Davies, S., 1996, *Big brother: Britain's web of surveillance and the new technological order*, Pan Books, London: 172.

57. Privacy Commissioner for Australia, December 1995, *Smart cards: implications for privacy*, Privacy Commissioner for Australia, Canberra: 15.

58. Central Computer and Telecommunications Agency

(CCTA), 1995, *Smart cards: opportunities for public sector applications*, HMSO, London: 6. Also 'Going for Olympic gold cards', *Economist*, 30.3.96, 89-90.

59. Schoechle, T.D., 1995, 'Privacy on the information superhighway', *Telecommunications Policy*, vol. 19 no. 6: 435-452.

60. The expression is that of Roland Moreno, widely regarded as the inventor of the technology that now supports smart cards.

61. Council of Europe, 1989, *New technologies: a challenge to privacy protection?*, Council of Europe, Strasbourg.

62. Louis Harris and Associates and Westin, A., 1994, *Equifax-Harris consumer privacy survey 1994*, Equifax, Atlanta, Georgia.

63. The Henley Centre for Forecasting, 1995, *Dataculture: privacy, participation and the need for transparency in the information age*, Henley Centre for Forecasting, London: ch. 4.

64. According to one historian of privacy, there was a time in almost all cultures when all behaviour was public behaviour. Only with the rise of industrial society did citizens start to take privacy for granted. Nock, S.I., 1993, *The costs of privacy: surveillance and reputation in America*, Aldine de Gruyter, New York.

65. Some of the many examples of these kinds of abuse in the US are documented in: Linowes, D.F., 1989, *Privacy in America: is your private life in the public eye?*, University of Illinois Press, Chicago; Rubin, M.R., 1988, *Private rights, public wrongs: the computer and personal privacy*, Ablex, New Jersey. Such fears have been expressed about multi-functional smart cards in particular, by the National Consumer Council, 1995, *Identity cards: response to the Home Office green paper*, National Consumer Council, London: 21-23.

66. Personal communication from the Office of the Data Protection Registrar; the data from this research have not been published.

67. Schoechle, T.D., 'Privacy on the Information Superhighway', *Telecommunications Policy*, vol. 19, no. 6, 435-452.

68. 'We know you're reading this', *The Economist* 10.2.96.

69. Linowes, D.F., 1989, *Privacy in America: is your private life in the public eye?*, University of Illinois Press, Chicago.

70. In 1983, the West German Constitutional Court found the Census Act unconstitutional, holding that 'The right to self-determination in relation to information precludes a social order and a legal order enabling it, in which citizens no longer can know who knows what, when and on what occasion about them. If someone is uncertain whether deviant behaviour is noted down and stored permanently as information, or is applied or passed on, he will not try to attract attention by such behaviour'. Michael, J., 1994, 'Privacy', in McCrudden, C. and Chambers, G., eds, 1994, *Individual rights and law in Britain*, Clarendon Press, Oxford: 268.

71. The case has been argued specifically about smart identity cards that have multiple applications by the Information and Privacy Commissioner for the Province of British Columbia, David H. Flaherty, 1995, *The problem with multi-purpose identity cards – the view from British Columbia*, Information and Privacy Commissioner for the Province of British Columbia, Victoria, British Columbia, Canada.

72. Wilson, K., 1988, *Technologies of control: the new interactive media for the home*, University of Wisconsin Press, Madison, Wisconsin, USA, cited in Schoechle, T.D., 1995, 'Privacy on the information superhighway', *Telecommunications Policy*, vol 19, no. 6, 435-452.

73. These range from crypto-anarchists such as Tim May to Privacy International activist, Simon Davies.

74. The development of separate codes of practice for each industry in North America is discussed in Raab, C.D., 1995, 'Connecting Orwell to Athens? Information superhighways and the privacy debate', in van de Donk, W., Snellen, I. and Tops, P., eds., 1995, *Orwell in Athens: a perspective on informatisation and democracy*, IOS Press, Amsterdam.

75. Liberty, 1995, *I-D cards: a solution looking for a problem*, Liberty, London: 2.

76. In Turkey, the mandatory identity card indicates the holder's religion, and is alleged to be punched with holes to indicate an ex-political prisoner; identity cards in Greece also indicate the holder's religion. It was even suggested in Britain in 1988 that identity cards should be issued and marked to indicate holders carrying the AIDS virus. Institute for Public Policy Research and Justice, 1995, *Identity cards revisited: a consultation paper*, IPPR and Justice, London: 17-18.

77. Institute for Public Policy Research and Justice, 1995, *Identity cards revisited: a consultation paper*, IPPR and Justice, London: 18.

78. Liberty, 1995, *I-D cards: a solution looking for a problem*, Liberty, London: 20-24.

79. A recent report revealed that computer hacking, theft and viruses are increasingly common in Whitehall. Instances of hacking have risen by 140 per cent since 1984, while viruses increased by

300 per cent: cited in Davies, S., 1996, *Big brother: Britain's web of surveillance and the new technological order*, Pan Books, London: 150.

80. Data Protection Registrar, 1995, *Identity cards: a consultation document*, Office of the Data Protection Registrar, Wilmslow.

81. Bondestam, A., 1993, 'Is it a sin to use a PIN?', excerpt from the proceedings of the XV International Conference of Data Protection and Privacy Commissioners.

82. One writer on privacy has commented that 'except to describe the underlying value, the term "privacy" ought to be resisted – especially as a legal term of art. It adds little to our understanding either of the interest that it sought to protect or of the conduct that it is designed to regulate'. Wacks, R., 1989, *Personal information: privacy and the law*, quoted in Michael, J., 'Privacy', in McCrudden, C. and Chambers, G., eds., 1994, *Individual rights and law in Britain*, Clarendon Press, Oxford.

83. Westin, A.F., 1967, *Privacy and freedom*, Athenaeum, New York: ch. 2.

84. Privacy has been seen by one author as a value 'like the dodo', which will be replaced by values of universal access and freedom in the information society. 'Private is history – get over it!' *Wired* magazine, February 96.

85. Westin, A.F., 1967, *Privacy and freedom*, Athenaeum, New York: chs. 2-4.

86. Enforcement of the consent principle has recently been taken by *The Economist* as the essence of any future strategy to protect privacy. 'Virtual Privacy', *The Economist,* 10.2.96.

87. Michael, J., 1994, 'Privacy', in McCrudden, C. and Chambers, G., eds, 1994, *Individual rights and law in Britain*, Clarendon Press, Oxford: 269. For a history of recent data protection and privacy policy, see Bennett, C.J., 1992, *Regulating privacy: data protection and public policy in Europe and the US*, Cornell University Press, New Jersey.

88. Office of the Data Protection Registrar, 1994, *Data Protection Act 1984: the Guidelines*, Office of the Data Protection Registrar, Wilmslow.

89. Commission of the European Communities, 1995, *Directive 95/46/EC of the European Parliament and of the Council of 24 October 1995 on the protection of individuals with regard to the processing of personal data and on the free movement of such data, Official journal of the European Communities*, Commission of the European Communities, Brussels, 24.10.95.

90. *R. v. Brown*, 8th February 1996, House of Lords.

91. Council of Europe, 1989,

New technologies: a challenge to privacy protection?, Council of Europe, Strasbourg.

92. Organisation for Economic Co-operation and Development, 1980, *Guidelines on the protection of privacy and transborder flows of personal data*, OECD, Paris; Council of Europe, 1981, Convention for the protection of individuals with regard to the automatic processing of personal data, Council of Europe, Strasbourg.

93. This is an acute problem, given the existence of many distributed and networked databases. Council of Europe, 1989, *New technologies: a challenge to privacy protection?*, Council of Europe, Strasbourg: 33.

94. Although in principle this should be corrected following implementation of the 1995 European Directive on data protection.

95. However, this is now changing in many countries, which are concentrating more on the processing of sensitive personal data. Michael, J., 1994, 'Privacy', in McCrudden, C. and Chambers, G., eds, 1994, *Individual rights and law in Britain*, Clarendon Press, Oxford: 281.

96. The US-based group, Computer Professionals for Social Responsibility, has been a leading light in promoting such technologies (their World Wide Web Site is at http://cpsr.org/). The Association of Computing Managers have also developed a code of ethics (see Redell, D., 1992, 'Draft ACM White Paper: information technology and the privacy of the individual', available from http://www.vortex.com/privacy/acm-wpd.1.Z).

97. Information and Privacy Commissioner, Ontario and Registratiekamer, 1995, *Privacy-enhancing technologies: the path to anonymity*, Vols I and II, Information and Privacy Commissioner, for Ontario and Registratiekamer, Ontario and Den Haag.

98. Chaum, D., 1992, 'Achieving electronic privacy', *Scientific American*, August, 96-102.

99. Information and Privacy Commissioner, Ontario and Registratiekamer, 1995, *Privacy-enhancing technologies: the path to anonymity*, Vols I and II, Information and Privacy Commissioner, Ontario and Registratiekamer, Den Haag: 9; 'Cash versus cashless', *Financial Times* 20.2.96.

100. Privacy Commissioner of Australia, 1995, *Smart cards: implications for privacy*, Privacy Commissioner for Australia, Canberra: 25.

101. This has recently been recommended by *The Economist* newspaper, 10.2.96: 16-17, and 51-

52.

102. Wright, T., 1993, *Smart cards, Information and Privacy Commissioner*, Ontario: 30.